THE SOUND OF BUSINESS

SEEING ENTREPRENEURSHIP *through* HIP HOP

TORI ELLIS

Tori Ellis
Brooklyn, New York

Book Coach – The Self-Publishing Maven
Cover Design – Okomota
Editing – Roseann Warren, The Edit Bae
Interior Layout – Chris P

ISBN: 978-17321564-0-1
LCCN: 2018914522

Printed in the United States of America

Acknowledgments

Thank you to my parents Troy and Karen, who showed me the 'love' in learning and understanding others. Thank you for being a guiding light of what it means to stay true to myself even in times of doubt.

I am truly grateful for all the family and friends that have been a part of my life's journey and continue to push me to strive far past any expectations.

Dear reader, continue to be the best you and always remember that passion, love, and continuous learning is always the path to unstoppable and undeniable growth. You heard!!

Contents

Introduction

In every organization there is a need for special individuals to come along and make it better. Now I don't intend to replace the CEO and run things yourself like you're the boss. But make the boss and organization better... provide that *GLOW UP*

For those of you who don't know what I'm talking about, the "glow up" is an urban slang term meaning amazing transformation. Now not all glow ups will be as amazing or as fast as others. But it is your duty as that Head Consultant to make them go as smoothly and effectively as possible. If you have that entrepreneurial spirit and feel that you can take it a step further to create a business of your own to target the needs of the community around you, go for it! There is nothing that can hold you back but yourself, it's time to take a chance. So, let's get to it...

This book isn't your ordinary cookie cutter book on Industrial Organizational Psychology. It's more like a compilation of all my greatest moments with hip-hop and how they influenced my outlook in Industrial Organizational Psychology and made me the businesswoman I am today. Industrial Organizational Psychology is the study of human behavior in the workplace and in an organization. Sounds boring, right? IOP is a complex study. TRUST ME! When I first took a course as a sophomore in college, I couldn't wrap my head around it. Way too much information was crammed into one class and the professor was a hard ass, so my frustration was at a high. By the time the middle of the semester rolled around, I was looking at the professor as if she had six heads. But now, let's just say I 'Bossed Up!'

The main reason I chose IOP was because of the variety of businesses I can aid with the knowledge and experience I've obtained over the years. Since IOP is distinctly focused on human behavior in work settings, the implementation and practice of it could be applied to different organizations across multiple markets (business, industry, labor, public, academic, community and health).

It's time to make some changes!

Pac speak to them...

CHANGES

"We gotta make a change
It's time for us as a people to start makin' some changes.
Let's change the way we eat, let's change the way we live
And let's change the way we treat each other.
You see the old way wasn't working so it's on us to do
What we gotta do, to survive."

– "Changes" by Tupac

The reason I wrote this book all started by my thesis for my master's degree, but later evolved into what I feel can help many millennials, like myself, really understand what it takes to be successful in organizations today or even in their own business. As you jump into the world of my personal experiences and influences with hip-hop, you might even recognize your own way of being an I/O consultant or even your own successful entrepreneur. For me it's simple: hip-hop, staying true to self, and knowledge. But everyone is different, and hip-hop is universal and present everywhere even when you don't expect it. With that said...

Yo turn the stereo up...

Beat drops

Hova Song (Intro) by Jay-Z starts to play in the background

Jay speaks

"Yeah, I know you just ripped the packaging off your CD
If you like me you reading the credits right now
If you in your car, I don't care if it's winter
I want you to put all your windows down
Zone out, buckle up, let's go."

CHAPTER 1

ORGANIZATIONAL THEORY AND BEHAVIOR

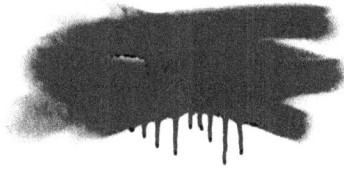

ip-hop as a whole is like any successful business that consistently evolves over time. It falls in line with the ever-changing demands of the people, as well as introducing future advancements. Hip-hop, one of the world's most successful genres, is nothing short of extraordinary. Its growth is always escalating to higher peaks and the evolution of hip-hop is ever-changing. In 1903, the first African American to earn a Ph.D. from Harvard University and popular civil rights activist/author, W.E.B. DuBois explored the concept of 'double consciousness'. This concept is a perfect description of hip-hop presently. Double consciousness describes the feeling as though one's identity is divided into several parts, leaving it difficult to identify by one unified identity. Hip-hop is far beyond just a genre of music, it is a culture. Hip-hop can be seen across different sources of expression (comedy, art, writing, music, and dance, etc.). It is beyond the rhythm and beats it presents.

Ironically, over time my love for hip-hop evolved just like my interest grew in business. Everything I've wanted to do, hip-hop was always close by. I can relate hip-hop to any business experience I've endured and relate to both organizational and industrial parts of a business. However, the empathy leans more towards the organization. I would even involve hip-hop or other outlets to connect with both internal and external customers. In order to understand how to run a successful business effectively, there is a history that can help.

Organizational Theory and Behavior

In the history of successful business management there are many theories that impact organizations. Organizational Theory is based on how an organization functions, the effects it has the environment around it, and the individuals working for the organization. According to MeanThat, an educational platform for business students focused on Marketing, Organizational Theory, and Business, organizations are made up of three areas: structure, culture, design, and change. Organizational structure is the formal system of task and authority relationships that control how people organize their actions and use resources to achieve organizational goals. On this level, it controls the organization's rules and consequences for not performing to set expectations. In hip-hop, the structure developed over time as it became more mainstream. The structure was considered the "grind" in which an artist had to find ways to present their artistry publicly. Some of these relationships, actions, and resources were very limited as well as crucial to the development and advancement of an artist. For example, if the artists did not build relationships with the local radio stations, or local vendors, the opportunity for their artistry to be discovered or even admired would be slim to none.

Organizational design and change is the process by which managers select and manage aspects of structure and culture so that an organization can control and monitor the activities necessary to achieve. During this level, managers delegate tasks to different teams to ensure every team is covering the functional areas of the organization to succeed. Hip-hop is based on design and change. It is commonly seen that the hitmakers are some of the most influential people in hip-hop because they provide guidance to new artists. Design and change are more prevalent in the music business as new artists are given the opportunity to venture from the expected sound to expand their creativity, thanks to their management.

Organizational Culture is the set of shared values and norms that control organizational members' interactions with each other, outside vendors, customers, and other people outside the organization. This is one of the most crucial levels of an organization because the culture of the organization affects different people within and outside of the company. Hip-hop is a culture. It affects many people on different levels and aspects of life. Hip-hop as a culture has been seen to bring together large groups of people for celebrations or just enjoying its relevance, for instance the BET Awards, the Hip Hop Hall of Fame Awards, and Summer Jam.

The organizational theory has changed over the years from rigid structures to flexible frameworks that change with the times. In Laurie Mullins' textbook Management & Organisational Behaviour, many topics are highlighted essential to any IOP student on the evolution of organizational theory, behavior, and management. The classical approach to organizational theory was, "criticised generally for not taking significant account of personality factor." During that time the personality and behavior of an employee weren't taken into consideration because companies viewed their employees as a means of production and income. The hip-hop group N.W.A., fought hard for their creative freedom and the ability to be valued as artists, while making a profit on their success. In the music industry, it is common to see independent artists who value their craft, and not want to have their music changed just to

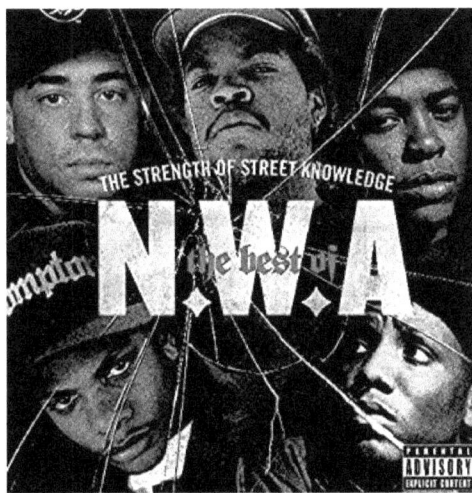

make ends meet. N.W.A. was one of those revolutionary groups who blatantly fought a system that disrespected them as artists.

This approach later evolved to focus on Human Relations, which are social factors in the work place such as in groups, leadership, informal organization, and behaviors of employees. According to Mullins, the classical approach adopted more of a managerial perspective, while the human relations approach strove for a greater understanding of people's psychological and social needs at work as well as improving the process of management. Seeing that human behavior plays a major factor in the success of a company, human relations movement brought on behaviorism. The behaviorism viewpoint stresses the importance of understanding the forces that influence individual employee behavior, mainly focusing on the individual employee's motivation to perform to their best ability. In hip-hop, the revolution began when artists rejected the music industry's restrictions and started to act on their right to artistic freedom. Some artists were seen to conform to the demands of their employers out of fear of losing their opportunities, while others fought against those demands and risked everything.

Over time the Systems Theory arose. The Systems approach was a blend of both the classical and human relations approach, where systems are put in place to control how the organization operates. Mullins noted that in this approach, "attention is focused on the total work organisation and the interrelationships of structure and behaviour, and the range of variables within the organisation." This later included the use of technology in the workplace to help teams, management, job satisfaction, and other forms of systems and structures. Some of the most prominent and influential music labels in the world converted their organization by mirroring the structured system of other companies before its time. The contingency theory came into play later to argue that not one approach is wrong or the best design for every organization. Mullins stated that, "the contingency approach implies that organisation theory should not seek to suggest one best way to structure or manage organisations but should provide insights into the situational and contextual factors which influence management decisions."

As time continued, flexibility became a key factor in all parts of an organization. Mullins gave some insight on the postmodernism approach, which describes organizations as, "highly flexible, free-flowing and fluid structures with the ability to change quickly to meet present demands." If a company has room to change with the demands of its environment, it will more likely be able to continue to be a profitable business. In a time where there is always constant competition and changes, postmodernism provides room for changes to meet the needs and demands of the environment.

In today's society, organizations worldwide have adopted a new theory called Holocracy. Holocracy is a flexible yet complex system of management in an organization that is designed so work can be completed faster with more clarity and more autonomy. In this style of management, it allows each employee to be self-aware and self-empowered (much like how hip-hop empowers people to express themselves in different forms of the art). Global business consultant, Steve Denning wrote in a Forbes magazine article, "Making Sense of Zappos and Holocracy," that although holocracy allows employees to be their own boss, in a sense it still has levels of hierarchy in its system that still holds some power over others. According to Denning, "there is a hierarchy of circles, which are to be run according to detailed democratic procedures… each higher circle tells its lower circle (or circles), what its purpose is and what is expected of it." Independent labels are a good present-day example of holocracy. Artists develop their creations with freedom and ease but there are still levels of procedures they must follow in order to complete tasks, get their music recognized, and placed on public platforms.

One of my all-time favorite hip-hop artists is Tupac Shakur, a great example of a misunderstood visionary. Shakur, one of the greatest rappers, poets, and actor, was a true artist of his own belief and individuality. He was born in East Harlem, New York, and made his mark as a West Coast artist. Shakur was noted for his many roles on the big screen alongside major heavy hitters in both the music and movie industry (Janet Jackson, Arthur Baylor, Bernie Mac, Marlon Wayans, Omar Epps, Queen Latifah, etc.) in movies like, Juice, Poetic Justice, Above the Rim, and Bullet, to name a few. In 1995, Shakur signed with Death Row Records, a label most notoriously known for its violent reputation. During his time Death Row Records, before his untimely death in 1996, Shakur (along with Snoop Dogg, who we will later talk about) was a staple in their continuous rise to recognition in the music industry especially for the West Coast. Along with success in music and media, came many different reputation issues/beefs that arose in Shakur's life that were publicly noted. In his music, you would hear about his passions and life struggles, but in his public persona during his time on Death Row Records, you would see someone portrayed in violence and often criticized ignorant behavior, which was heavily associated with his label at this time. This is a perfect example of where organizational behavior was evident. So now let's break down Organizational behavior.

Organizational behavior is how personnel react and adapt to the changes within an organization and the structure it upholds. It is very important to understand organizational behavior because each individual in the organization has their own personality, strengths, and weaknesses. In order to fully succeed, it is imperative that a leader knows the personality, strengths, and weaknesses of each employee to help them build relationships to gain respect and trust. When an employee is supported by their leader, they are more likely to be open to feedback and work their hardest to meet expectations. Without understanding behavior and personality, a leader will not be able to know how to motivate their employees.

Individual Behavior

Importance of Organizational Behaviour

Through Organizational Behaviour a Manager can know..

➤ How to Motivate subordinates
➤ How to lead
➤ Attitude of workers
➤ Value system
➤ Methods of Enhance Job Satisfaction
➤ How to Develop Team spirit
➤ How to solve disputes

Some of the common examples of individual behaviors in society, hip-hop, and business seen are accepting, passing, and revealing behaviors. To identify what kind of employee you are encountering, there are a few traits each of them has:

- **Accepting**: Accepters prioritize their work identities and sacrifice or significantly suppress other meaningful aspects of their true selves. These types of employees bring both pros and cons to an organization. On the pros side, you have individuals who are dedicated to being successful in their jobs and strive to reach set expectations. However, with this kind of pressure it can wear down on the employee causing stress and anxiety if the job cannot be completed. Also, if this worker is of a leadership rank, when it is time to help another employee, their own expectations take precedence, leaving the subordinate to fend for themselves. They are solely consumed in their job and not all employees are willing to sacrifice all their personal time for a job. If the job is stressful, and they are not satisfied with their job, it can cause them to underperform in their duties below expectation.

- **Passing:** In this type of behavior, employees find time to indulge in their personal activities outside of work and keep these activities to themselves. It is almost as if they follow that saying, "Keep business and pleasure separate." However, passers pay a psychological price for hiding parts of themselves. These employees are relatively protecting their image, so they may not build close relationships at work. In a thriving organization, communication and team building are essential. If employees are not communicating with one another and building a team that is reliable and on task, it can damage an organization's structure.

- **Revealing:** In this type of behavior employees' risk of damaging their image and dedication to a company by openly revealing they have other priorities outside of work. If their manager or leadership team consists of people looking for dedicated individuals and they are not willing to give up personal time for work, their work ethic and credibility may be questioned. This type of stress on an employee can cause unhappiness and bring down the morale in the company. All good leaders show support for their employees. If their leader is not supportive of their actions, it can leave them to question themselves and their ability to complete their job. Over time, being sanctioned for failure to conform can lead to resentment and can cause employees to leave the organization.

In hip-hop, many artists live public, revealing lives. Others like singer, rapper, songwriter, record and film producer, Pharrell Williams, is known to keeping his family life private and separate from his business life. However, these differences do not seem to hinder hip-hop lovers like myself from falling in love with particular artists and connecting to their creations. There is a combination of things that describe what it means to be hip-hop: the people, the understanding of the music, the expansions of, and the common struggle for survival that is often portrayed. The depth of hip-hop is the feeling, passion, and love for hip-hop and its culture. People in hip-hop appreciate the versatility it holds, they listen to the tone, the beat, the story, and the flow of each emcee. Whether it's the wordplay of Chino XL and Eminem or the imagery and personification that Common so perfectly puts together; people that live hip-hop notice and appreciate every aspect of hip-hop. Understanding the styles of hip-hop such as scratching, sampling, the importance of the DJ and the emcee also play a huge part in hip-hop culture because that is the basis of the music and how it has evolved. Most important is the story each emcee projects to his audience, whether targeting specific topics like sex, race, discrimination, relationships or creating a poetic combination of musical genres and metaphors to show life as a whole like New York City rapper, Nas has done in his work. However, in order to survive in hip-hop or in any workplace, there are different individual behavioral factors that are important. Tayla Bauer and Berrin Erdogan, two award-winning professors who specialize in lecturing on organizational behavior, management, and human resources, among other topics, wrote, An Introduction to Organizational Behavior, which provides a solid foundation and breakdown of organizational behavior. With their help, I was able to understand many concepts of IOP that I first found difficult in college.

With the help of Bauer and Erdogan, let's break down the three most important individual behavioral factors:

Congratulations on still fitting into your work pants.

som[ee]cards

Making sure the person best fits the job. According to Bauer and Erdogan, "Person-job fit is the degree to which a person's skill, knowledge, ability, and other characteristics match the job demands. It is a manager's duty to set employees up for success. When an employee has confidence and feels comfortable in the job they are in, they perform to the best of their ability. It is important to place employees in positions that match their abilities and give them expectations that they can reach that also challenge them to enhance their skills.

Making sure the person has strong personality traits that fit for the job. Looking for individuals who carry what is considered great traits for any business, usually possess two of the Big Five Personality Traits. These traits are beneficial in different areas of an organization. The first personality trait of conscientiousness is being organized, systematic, punctual, achievement-oriented, and dependable. These are employees who are organized and systematic, are willing to handle a lot of information, clients inside and outside of the business, and are always ready to better themselves. The second personality trait is agreeableness, the degree to which a person is nice, tolerant, sensitive, trusting, kind, and warm. These are employees who do not have a problem communicating with clients and helping them with any of their problems and concerns. This would allow a sense of trust to build between client and employee. Agreeable people help others at work consistently, and this helpful behavior is not dependent on being in a good mood, it's just their nature.

Making sure the person has a proactive personality. According to Bauer and Erdogan, proactive people take the initiative to make meaningful change and remove the obstacles they face along the way. After careful observation of society and the consistent change in consumer demands, having solution-based people on your team is crucial. They make a difference in your team when problems arise at the last minute.

These individual behavioral factors also roll over into leadership traits and styles in successful organizations. Of course, each trait works better and differently for each individual. Hip-hop is the same in that each tone or beat, or even each topic may affect each individual differently.

Leadership Traits and Styles

Leadership traits that will motivate individuals, teams, and groups would be intelligence, Big Five Personality Traits, Self Esteem, and Integrity. The intelligence and general ability of a leader are very important to the success of an organization because they are making major decisions that will affect many levels of business. In hip-hop, being a leader is one of the main traits of the artist — their knowledge of their audience and what is being expected of them as public figures affect their business.

The Big Five Personality Traits are commonly used to focus on specific traits that organizations look for in employees based on the jobs they are applying for. Subconsciously, I questioned if these traits applied to artists when they are being scouted for record deals. Since the music industry is a business, they look for products they can sell. In hip-hop, artists are the creators and the products.

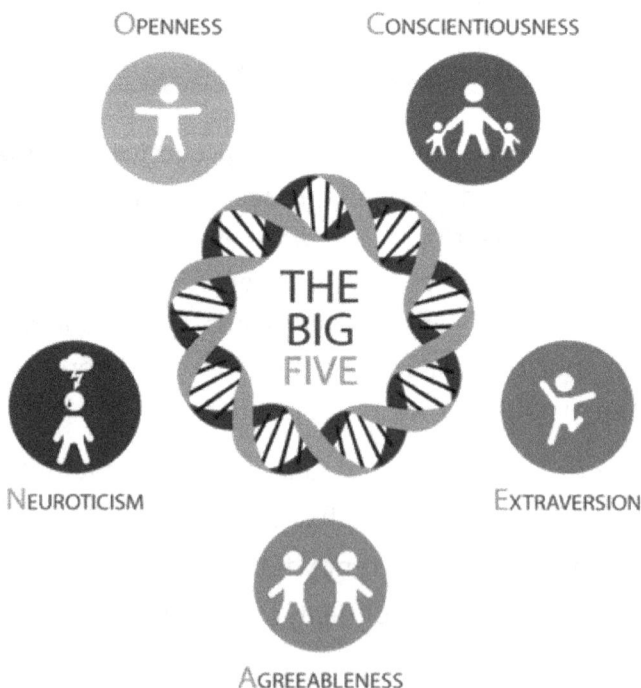

OPENNESS

CONSCIENTIOUSNESS

THE
BIG
FIVE

NEUROTICISM

EXTRAVERSION

AGREEABLENESS

The Big Five Personality Traits are openness, conscientiousness, extraversion, agreeableness, and neuroticism. However, only four of these traits are ideal leadership traits to motivate employees.

Bauer and Erdogan state that, openness is the ability to "be curious, original, intellectual, creative, and open to new ideas." A trait like openness can be very effective in organization fields like think tanks, scientists, and creative fields. This trait in a leader allows the ability for open communication with their team, which can lead to forming new ideas and positive feedback. In hip-hop, openness is necessary in order to give and receive feedback or critiques. Conscientiousness is the ability to "be organized, systematic, punctual, achievement-oriented, and dependable." This trait in a leader is crucial because they are dealing with many different teams and personalities. They need to be able to delegate tasks based on expertise as well as having organized information to support their staff. Extraversion is the ability to "be outgoing, talkative, sociable, and enjoying social situations." Extraverts are commonly seen in fields that deal with a lot of people like talk show hosts, sales associates, etc. Leaders with this trait can motivate their staff by connecting more on a personal level and use different avenues to reach the interests of their staff outside of the workplace. Hip-hop is filled with artists who are extroverts and motivate their audience on personal levels. Agreeableness is the ability to "be affable, tolerant, sensitive, trusting, kind, and warm." Leaders with this trait have the ability to connect with their staff and show empathy. They care more for the emotional needs of their staff and are open to listening and providing support. Finally, neuroticism is "being anxious, irritable, temperamental, and moody." This personality trait is not an ideal trait for any business leader because it can cause a lot of problems and tension amongst staff, leaders, and customers. In hip-hop, on the other hand, many artists fuel their creations or even their personality on this trait.

Self-esteem in leadership is crucial as the staff following must follow a leader who is confident in the vision they see for their organization. Hip-hop embodies self-esteem. Bauer and Erdogan state that leaders with high self-esteem support their team members more, and when punishment is administered, they punish more effectively. Finally, integrity is a trait that a leader should possess because they have a moral code in which to follow and ensure honesty and trustworthiness. When a leader's integrity or intelligence is in question, they are being tested on their trustworthiness and knowledge of their organization, which can lead to many problems down the line. In organizations, in hip-hop, and in society there are different levels of interactions amongst people: individuals, teams, and groups. Leadership styles can work for each level:

Individuals

People-oriented leader behaviors include showing concern for employee feelings and treating employees with respect. This kind of leadership is beneficial to motivating individuals as these leaders build personal relationships with their employees and help them excel in areas they may lack. Supportive leaders help employees on many levels aside from just work. They are focused on their emotional state and are encouraging. Achievement-oriented leaders are beneficial in motivating their staff by setting goals for each employee and encouraging them to achieve it. Every staff member is unique and has their own set of goals that relate to them both outside and inside of work.

Teams

Directive leaders lead employees by clarifying role expectations, setting schedules, and making sure that employees know what to do on a day-to-day basis. With direction, teams can be more efficient and can save time implementing changes instead of trying to figure out what expectations need to be met. Participative leaders are great in motivating team members because they make sure their members are involved in making important decisions.

Groups

Task-oriented leader behaviors involve structuring the roles of subordinates, providing them with instructions, and behaving in ways that will increase the performance of the group. This leadership style would be beneficial for groups because it focuses on changes that will increase its performance and structure roles. Transformational leader style is motivating to groups because it helps transform the employee goals to align with the leader's goal for the organization. Employees will stop focusing on individual needs and focus on the well-being of the organization.

Organizational Culture

Organizational Culture lays the groundwork for how an organization is run and the mission of it. Organizational culture is the root cause and effect of how an organization excels. According to Bauer and Erdogan, "An organization's culture may be one of its strongest assets, as well as its biggest liability." As I stated before, hip-hop is a culture.

This culture is formed in various ways just as organizational culture. In order to identify, measure, and manage organizational culture effectively, identifying a set of values may help. In an organization's culture, there are three levels: assumptions, values, and artifacts. A leader can use assumptions, values, and artifacts to better an organization's culture by finding the weak spots in its structure, thereby strengthening it. In an organization, having the assumption that behavior would relate to the outcome of organizational progression or downfall could make or break a leader. If a leader assumes wrong about their culture, they can miss room for change that can ultimately benefit them. Bauer and Erdogan summed up values as shared principles, standards, and goals.

Three Levels of Culture (Schein)

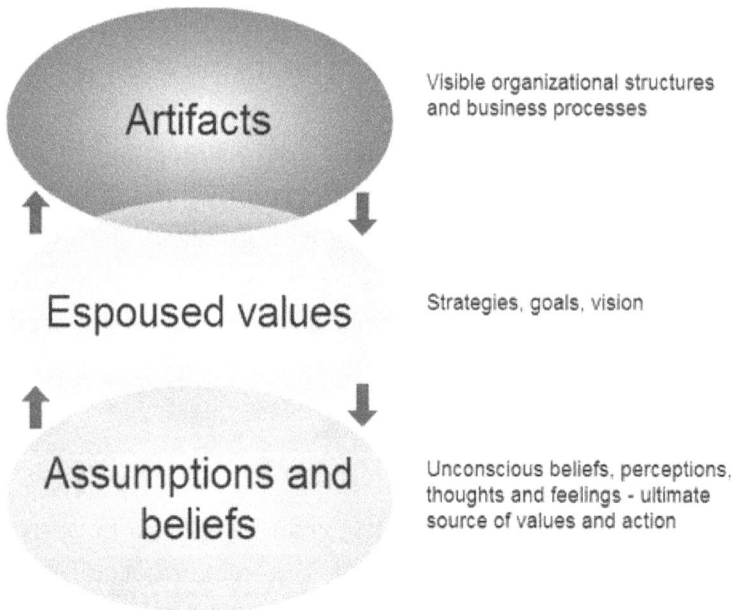

Artifacts

Visible organizational structures and business processes

Espoused values

Strategies, goals, vision

Assumptions and beliefs

Unconscious beliefs, perceptions, thoughts and feelings - ultimate source of values and action

The order of the organization depends on values. If these are not communicated, it leaves room for errors to occur amongst staff and leadership. The leader must communicate these values by demonstrating the behavior in order to be effective. The artifacts important to a leader are observable characteristics that can be measured. With this information, a leader can gain direction of the organization and make changes in times of need, so the organization can continue to progress without major setbacks.

There are many dimensions to organizational culture. Each dimension is based on characteristics and a set of values that are used to describe that culture. According to the Organizational Culture Profile below, there are seven distinct values: innovative, aggressive, outcome-oriented, stable, people-oriented, team-oriented, and detail oriented.

Organizational Culture Profile

Org Culture Dimensions	Dimension Characteristics
Innovation	Experimenting, opportunity seeking, risk taking, few rules, low cautiousness
Stability	Predictability, security, rule-oriented
Respect for people	Fairness, tolerance
Outcome orientation	Action oriented, high expectations, results oriented
Attention to detail	Precise, analytic
Team orientation	Collaboration, people-oriented
Aggressiveness	Competitive, low emphasis on social responsibility

Organizational culture is the root cause and effect of how an organization excels. The culture of an organization sets the tone for the employees to follow as well as alter during change processes.

Hip-Hop Leadership

Hip-hop originated in the streets and ghettos of New York City in the 1970s. Hip-hop embodies the true culture and spirit of strength, courage, and struggle. Many people involved in the hip-hop culture use hip-hop to express the many struggles of life, and the courage and strength it takes to overcome those adversities. Hip-hop is a global multi-billion-dollar culture that comes in many art forms (music, theater, film, entrepreneurship, language, fashion, knowledge, etc.). Valerie Patterson, a Ph.D. recipient from the University of Delaware, conducted research on the evolution of leaders and leadership in Hip-Hop culture, and the implications offered for leading a diverse workforce. She called it, "Engaging Hip-Hop Leadership: Diversity, Counter-Hegemony and Glorified Misogyny (Free-Style Version)." This study caught my eye for several reasons, but mainly on how she broke down lyrics from hip-hop songs to explain the major points of her study (you will find many lyrics from a few of my favorite artists throughout this book as well).

In the study, Patterson spoke about how hip-hop is being recognized as a culture that can be useful in concepts of leadership. Several hip-hop industry leaders have been successful in influencing generations of consumers in embracing the culture. Hip-hop has many different leaders who are influential in different categories. These categories include politics, law, business, arts and entertainment, public service, and the new power.

One of the influential businessmen Patterson highlighted was Jay-Z aka Shawn Carter and what she described as the Shawn 'Jay-Z' Carter Leadership Model. "Jay-Z's success suggests that hip-hop culture offers a model of counter-hegemony that has forced corporate America to embrace nontraditional models of business leadership... In assessing the intersection between hip-hop culture and leadership models, one can conclude that the decision to appoint Shawn "Jay-Z" Carter as CEO reflects an increased understanding of the importance of innovation and creativity and how each of these elements come together to impact the bottom-line."

Type of Leadership	Effective Attributes
Structural	Analyst, Architect
Human Resource	Catalyst, Servant
Political	Advocate, Negotiator
Symbolic	Prophet, Poet

After Patterson broke down his background for leadership traits, it was concluded that he combines both structural and symbolic leadership styles with some skills in the political frame (see chart for the list of effective attributes of a leader). His style is also connected to a combination of traditional attributes of leadership and attributes of transformational leadership. Jay-Z's leadership styles proved to benefit him as one of hip-hop's greatest icons. His success as a leader is reflected in the recent news that he has entered into a deal to sell his clothing company Rocawear for $204 million in cash to Iconix Brand Group, the company that licenses and markets Candies, Joe Boxer, Mudd, London Fog, and Ocean Pacific. His brand continues to grow as he tackles different business ventures and initiatives to motivate people around the world.

CHAPTER 2

FACILITATING ORGANIZATIONAL CHANGE

the originator | late 80s | the conscious rapper | the east coast thug | dirty south bling bling | hipster rap

> "A-yes, yes y'all, and you don't stop
>
> To the beat, y'all, and you don't stop
>
> Yes, yes, y'all, and you don't stop
>
> A-one, two, y'all, and you don't stop
>
> A-yes, yes y'all, and you don't stop
>
> And to the beat Com Sense'll be the sure shot, come on"
>
> —"I Used To Love H.E.R." by Common

"I Used to Love H.E.R." greatly describes a love for hip-hop, both good and bad. Common, a hip-hop recording artist, actor, poet, and film producer, lyrically took us on a ride through the beautiful evolution of hip-hop as he personifies H.E.R. (Hip-Hop in its Essence is Real) as a woman he used to love who has undergone different phases in her life (specifically the transition from conscious rap to the east coast, G Funk, and other main-stream rap). Facilitating organizational change is no different to hip-hop, especially in transitioning a change to become a more mainstream and consumer-based organization. In "I Used to

Love H.E.R.," Common portrays both high and low parts of hip-hop, and explains how the change happened, the loss of purity in the culture, and quality over time due to commercialism, but nonetheless hip-hop is still his love that still hits his soul, and he will fight to bring her back to glory. In organizational change, one needs to understand what hits the soul and how to allow it to benefit you, but also understand the need for stability.

Change Signature

In the previous chapter, we briefly touched on the leadership style of Jay-Z. Over the years of learning and being independent in the work force, I have realized over time my purpose. My change signature is that of a Change Agent. Being in a managerial role, where I am able to implement change in my workplace, I help to grow and expand the brand. I'm always up to the challenge of creating a vision, making the steps necessary to succeed, and maintain the change after it has occurred. I am not a change agent who is closed off to the opinions of others, in fact, I am very open to listening to how others view the company and the changes that need to be made on their behalf.

Leadership Skills for Change

The leadership skills I've seen common amongst myself, Jay-Z, and even hip-hop are summed up in these four points: envisioning, motivating, team building, and communication. Common spoke about the many attributes of hip-hop in his lyrics. He used metaphors and envisioning skills to provide us with hip-hop's story into the 90s. Now let's set the tone for hip-hop as we break down each leadership skill for change in detail:

"I met this girl when I was 10 years old
And what I loved most she had so much soul
She was old school when I was just a shorty
Never knew throughout my life she would be there for me

On the regular, not a church girl, she was secular
Not about the money, those studs was mic-checkin' her
But I respected her, she hit me in the heart
A few New York niggas had did her in the park
But she was there for me, and I was there for her
Pull out a chair for her, turn on the air for her
And just cool out, cool out, and listen to her

Sittin' on a bone, wishin' that I could do her
Eventually if it was meant to be, then it would be
'Cause we related, physically and mentally
And she was fun then, I'd be geeked when she'd come around
Slim was fresh, yo, when she was underground
Original, pure, untampered, a down sister
Boy, I tell you, I miss her."

Envisioning: By creating a vision, the leader provides a vehicle for people to develop commitment, a common goal around which people can rally, and a way for people to feel successful. With this leadership skill, you are providing your team with a sense of purpose and holding them accountable for their actions and progression in the company. Ideally, I have learned that when you keep your vision true to yourself and your organization's mission, it is easier to achieve. In Common's first verse, (see above) he reminisces about hip-hop's untampered, down to earth, and pure demeanor in the underground era. Many times, when organizations go through expansions, they may encounter a little struggle during transitions, and after it all you are left with a 50/50 outcome: either push through and make it on top or lose quality due to globalization.

"Now periodically I would see
Ol' girl at the clubs, and at the house parties
She didn't have a body, but she started gettin' thick quick
Did a couple of videos and be-came Afrocentric
Out goes the weave, in goes the braids, beads, medallions
She was on that tip about stoppin' the violence
About my people she was teachin' me
By not preachin' to me but speakin' to me
In a method that was leisurely, so easily I approach
She dug my rap, that's how we got close."

In his lyrics, Common speaks on how hip-hop started to evolve into a new entity, one which motivated the people to what she was speaking too. This leads us into the leadership skill of motivating. **Motivating:** A leader who motivates their team produces positive morale and makes them want to work harder towards a goal. They find and use success to celebrate progress towards the vision. Common described this phase in hip-hop (see part of verse 2 above) as she spoke to him about the change of his culture. The era of hip-hop Common raps about, female rappers like Queen Latifah, MC Lyte, and Monie Love, were using their voices to rap about the problems such as violence in the community, taking a feminist stance. Hip-hop was used to motivate the people by informing them of the struggles and hardships that were taking place in the urban communities. It was not until later that hip-hop would spread awareness worldwide.

Alongside the motivating leadership skill, there is the enabling skill which goes hand in and. **Enabling:** A leader providing personal support, empathy, and expressing confidence towards employees enforces a level of concern about everyone's needs and pushes them to surpass their goals. It is an effective leadership skill for change because oftentimes, employees lose momentum or feel discouraged.

But then she broke to the West Coast, and that was cool
Cause around the same time, I went away to school
And I'm a man of expandin', so why should I stand in her way?
She probably get her money in L.A.

And she did stud, she got big pub, but what was foul
She said that the pro-black was goin' out of style
She said, "Afrocentricity was of the past"
So she got into R&B, hip-house, bass, and jazz
Now black music is black music and it's all good I wasn't salty,
she was with the boys in the hood
Cause that was good for her, she was becomin' well- rounded
I thought it was dope how she was on that freestyle shit
Just havin' fun, not worried about anyone
And you could tell by how her titties hung."

Team Building: It is important to have team building skills to help build structures that can help the company produce great outcomes. No matter how capable or dedicated the leader is, groups without strong line leadership never achieve the power that is required. Team building is key to an organization as the goal is to a strong dependable team. In hip-hop, the expansion was huge. It started in the borough of the Bronx, and grew internationally, forty years and counting. Common described hip-hop's evolution with the West Coast rappers, and their style of flow and presentation. Da Brat, a female rapper and actress of the 1990s was one of the first female rappers to be known as a member of the LGBTQ community, publicly. Hip-hop has now expanded its scope into styles of R&B, hip-house, bass, jazz, and pop music. Of course, with expansion leads to cause for resistance, however, all change does.

As a change agent or any form of leader and/or team member, it is very important to utilize multiple forms of communication. As a change agent, one must be able to vocalize and demonstrate what is expected of their team members.

Communication: Communication is necessary for change to occur because employees must understand the vision that is trying to be accomplished, as well as see their leader model the behavior and expectations required for what is to be accomplished. Communication comes in both words and actions, and the latter is often the most powerful form. Some of the major concerns when communicating a message before and during the implementation of a change project is:

- **Promoting communication and participation:** Before a change project can begin, the leader must express the new vision they have, what they need, who they need in order for this change to happen successfully, and when the change will begin. As part of the change agents' role in promoting communication and participation, they give other organizational members the necessary resources to conduct the change process. If the message is unclear, it can cause confusion in the organization and potential errors can occur.

- **Facilitating the change communicated project:** During this process the leader can help guide their staff on the next steps needed to complete the change, and delegate different tasks for each team member. Leaders can take different opinions from fellow staff members for ideas on how to complete the change as well.

- **Supporting the communicated message:** To enforce the change, continuous forms of communication is crucial. Pathways of communication must always be open. It is commonly seen that if the communicated message is not followed with proper support (follow-up meetings, memos, etc.) staff sometimes will sway away from the vision. Face-to-face interactions tend to have the best effect on supportive forms of communication.

Managing Change

In order to change the organization for the better, I had to first understand what exactly was wrong with the business and then create a plan to initiate the change. When going over the problems in the business, I looked for what I needed in order to make it successful:

the environmental forces = what environmental factors affect the business marketplace requirements = what are the requirements for similar businesses in that area business imperatives = important goals of the business

organizational imperatives = important goals of the organization cultural imperatives = important goals of job culture

leader and employee behavior = the expected behavior of the leaders and employee's leader and employee mindset = the expected mindset of the leaders and employees

When you can pinpoint the driver of change (the reason the change was initiated), it can be easier to create a plan to solve the problem at hand. In order to ensure success in my change implementation, I found these key components the most beneficial:

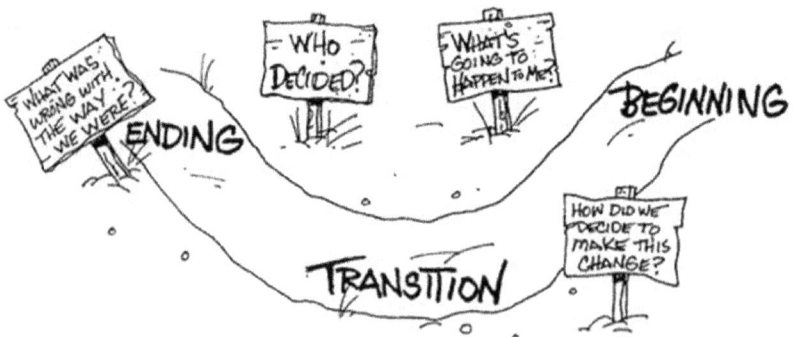

Creating a vision: Leaders must encourage the organization to take a hard look at which functions, geographies, or product lines to change or enforce. At times when changes need to be made within a company, managers often create expectations that are not attainable due to lack of clear vision for what needs to be done or have insufficient support to do so. Suitable mission statements backed up by organization values and making available the resources required for achieving change is the fundamental quality of achieving the desired vision.

Managing the transition: This is the most important step. It includes the plans for what is needed and how it should be executed to complete the transition. It involves preparing a checklist of various activities, a sequence of events, and people responsible for various activities. It involves the support and commitment of the key members in the organization whose leadership, resources, and energy are crucial to the success of transition. The transition should always have a steady pace to it. For the transition to progress it must stay on the path and push through every stepping stone it may face because it's evolving into something new. Giving different jobs to different groups of employees will have a bigger impact on how the company will grow. A smaller set of high-impact, brisk-moving initiatives are more energizing—and thus more sustainable—than a broader set of initiatives moving at a slow-moving pace.

Sustaining Momentum: As changes start to occur, maintaining the same amount of effort and energy the employees had when the change started is crucial. Providing resources for change, building a support system for the change agent, developing new competencies and skills, and reinforcing new behaviors are all elements needed to sustain momentum during the transition. Without any of these elements working in tandem, momentum can die down and many unforeseen circumstances can occur. Employees must focus on sustaining the vision once it starts to take shape. New vision comes with a new way of execution and a new system, which means it becomes easy access for errors to arise and cause disruption in the transition process. If employees do not see a change over time or feel like they can't achieve the vision, they may feel discouraged, and would need their leader to guide and support them to reinforce motivation and push them to achieve their goals.

In hip-hop, changes were seen over a period as it started to evolve and include other genres of music, and other elements of the hip-hop culture. During certain eras in the hip-hop community, the transition was not always smooth, and the changes were quick and fast-paced. To be deemed a staple of the hip-hop community (for instance, the transition in the musicalstyle of hip-hop), the transition needed a lot of support and momentum from other artists and supporters of the hip-hop community.

Errors made during Change Process

Mistakes that I have seen to be very common in the workplace is when employers lack in critical areas of leadership and business acumen. In the case of hip-hop, the conflict arose among the different groups (between record labels). The most notorious rivalry was between the East Coast and West Coast hip-hop scenes, the battle between Death Row Records (West Coast) and Bad Boy Records (East Coast). The battle escalated further between Tupac and the Notorious B.I.G., which resulted in both of their deaths by unknown gunmen.

In reality, both sides failed to see the overall goal of the culture of hip-hop, which is uniting different people from around the world. West Coast rappers made popular thug life/violence portrayal in their music, whereas the management of these artists was directing and supporting them to create more music to become more mainstream and profitable, causing an increase in competition. Now, let's be clear, the Death Row change was very profitable and very popular, which is a positive. However, the major negative is the resulting deaths of two major staples in the hip-hop community. When large organizations are implementing changes to their structure, that can make or break their company, it is commonly seen that many mistakes are made. These mistakes are as follows:

> **Making unrealistic expectations:** When trying to attain a vision, some managers may expect change quickly instead of it gradually happening over time. They may also make expectations that are not attainable. As a manager you must be a role model and show the expectations that you want from your employees. If the leader cannot live up to the expectations they created for their team members, this can backfire.

> **Not creating a solid group to lead:** If the team you have put together isn't strong enough to lead the change, the initiative will be unsuccessful. Without a strong team leader this change will fail.

> **Not having proper communication:** If the team leader does not express the vision of the change, the expectations, and consequences of the change clearly, they run the risk of confusing staff. The leader must express the expectation as well as model the behavior required for their staff to lead successful change. Without credible communication, and a lot of it, the hearts and minds of the staff are never won over.

As a business owner, you can avoid the above errors by carefully planning your vision, how to execute it, and knowing who and what is needed in order to accomplish the change, successfully.

Also, going mainstream can cause negative effects on an organization. Many small businesses would heavily consider mainstreaming or commercializing their organization with fear that their product or organizational structure might lose its quality. "Quantity over quality" can become an issue. For instance, going mainstream may involve a change of culture. In order to adhere to different circumstances of the regional placement, environmental needs and demands, and/or new management, the original culture of the organization may change. In his final verse of "I Used to Love H.E.R.," Common concluded to the effects of mainstream on hip-hop. He illustrated how the demands of commercialism altered the original, raw demeanor of hip-hop to appease and submit to the new demands of what the community and record labels liked in order to turnover a profit. Common no longer saw the quality in hip-hop that he grew to love.

"I might've failed to mention
that this chick was creative
Once the man got to her, he altered he native
Told her if she got an image and a gimmick
That she could make money,
Now I see her in commercials, she's universal
She used to only swing it with the inner-city circle
Now she be in the burbs,
lookin' rock and dressin' hippie
And on some dumb shit when she comes
to the city

Talkin' bout poppin' Glocks, servin' rocks and hit-
tin' switches
Now she's a gangsta rollin' with gangsta bitches
Always smokin' blunts and gettin' drunk
Tellin' me sad stories,
now she only fucks with the funk
Stressin' how hardcore and real she is
She was really the realest,
before she got into showbiz
I did her, not just to say that I did it
But I'm committed (girl, he's committed)
but so many niggas hit it
That she's just not the same lettin' all these group-
ies do her
I see niggas slammin' her,
and takin' her to the sewer
But I'ma take her back, hopin' that the shit stop
'Cause who I'm talkin' about, y'all, is hip-hop."
Common "I Used to Love H.E.R."

Barriers and Resistance to Change

Hip-hop embodies the definition of resistance and change. One of the main barriers and resistance in hip-hop is its transition to the mainstream. Russell Simmons, a hip-hop mogul, entrepreneur, producer, and author is one of the first to push through the barriers of taking hip-hop music mainstream. As an African-American male, this alone put many delays and set backs on his endeavors, however he pushed through and succeeded in many different business ventures with the help of Rick Ruben.

He was a true man of his beliefs and stuck to what he aspired to do. Simmons said in an interview, "My experiences have been, from the very beginning, cultural and creative, and my business has been a way of exposing the culture, exposing the artists so that the world could hear and see them."

A common theme in Russell Simmons' struggle into the mainstream was larger companies trying to silence his businesses. A prime example could be seen during his transition to mainstream television, showing the world black comedic talent. Now let's switch it up. In the business world, employee silence is a major problem due to many factors. It illustrates a growing problem in an organization due to factors like the lack of trust and understanding amongst leaders and staff. Employees tend to silence themselves in order to avoid conflict or fear of the consequences that come with them stating their opinion. Some of the beliefs that lead to employee silence are:

Managers Fear of Negative Feedback: Many managers feel a strong need to avoid embarrassment, threat, and feelings of vulnerability or incompetence. Managers always want to show that they have control over the situation at hand, and never want to be questioned about their course of action. When challenged, sometimes they become defensive and block the information given or attack the person giving feedback. If they are receiving feedback from a subordinate, they may feel it threatens their power.

Managers Implicit Beliefs: Many managers believe that they know best, and that unity is good, and dissent is bad. If managers feel that they know what is best for the organization, they are not open to hearing ideas that might benefit or improve their original plan. Managers feel that they are in the leadership role so they must lead and the employees under them must follow. Secondly, they feel that unity is good. Unity, agreement, and consensus are signs of organizational health, whereas disagreement and dissent should be avoided, but sometimes can be healthy if properly monitored. If an organization is not unified and working as one, it may cause conflict in the progression of success. Managers would feel that disagreement may cause conflict and separation amongst staff.

As a manager you should allow feedback from your employees as this opens doors for better communication and a positive environment. Team members may have some ideas that you might not have thought of that can benefit the organization. Feedback is also beneficial to the role of a manager. All opinions are important. Feedback can be used to implement new ideas or even new methods into the coaching and training style of a manager and those under them. Disagreements challenge team members to think beyond their comfort zone, which can strengthen individuals and the team as a collective.

Resistance to change happens for many reasons, however it is commonly seen that resistance can stem from the uncertainty in the change. People also resist change when they do not understand its implications and perceive that it might cost them much more than they will gain. If the staff does not understand or trust their leader resistance may occur. Another resistance stems from different assessments of the change. A common reason people resist organization change is that they assess the situation differently from their managers, those who will be affected by the change have the same information. If staff and leader are not looking at the situation from the same viewpoint there can be different outlooks on what may actually happen. This may cause a rift in communication because there are multiple perceptions about the situation.

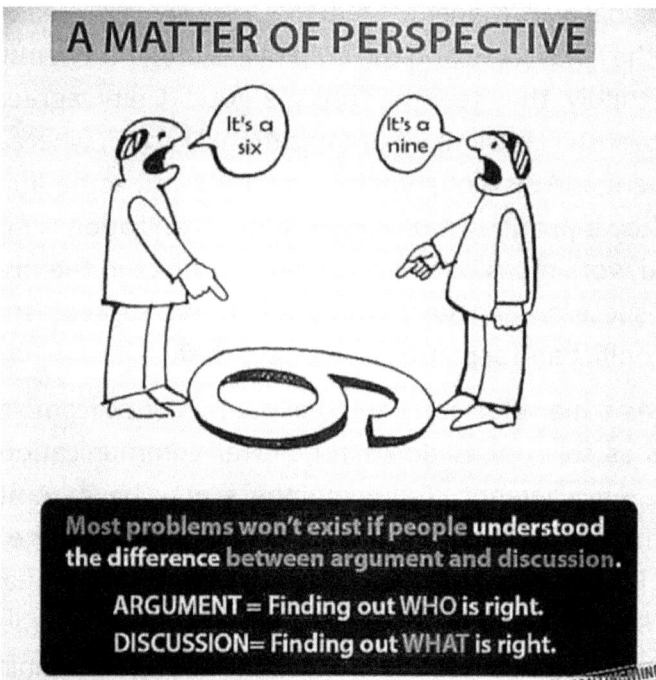

A MATTER OF PERSPECTIVE

It's a six

It's a nine

Most problems won't exist if people understood the difference between argument and discussion.

ARGUMENT = Finding out WHO is right.
DISCUSSION= Finding out WHAT is right.

Ambivalence can be seen in many situations especially when a member of the team is conflicted about the impending change. A leader can recognize ambivalence in their staff through attitudes and emotions during the change process. Some staff may show enthusiasm in the change but emotionally they experience fear because of the uncertainty in what the change may bring. An employee's response along the emotional dimension might range from strong positive emotions (such as excitement or happiness) to strong negative emotions (such as anger or fear).

A strategy that can be implemented when trying to prevent resistance is through participation and involvement. As a leader you must constantly reiterate the expectations of the vision and be a role model to your employees. In order to embrace ambivalence, open the doors for communication, while being transparent, showing the pros and cons of the change process, giving solid groundwork on how cons can be avoided, and leaving your staff with a clear state of mind to see the vision and its benefits.

Conclusion

Although these changes will bring about significant effects, these are just better representations or reincarnations of history. Wyclef Jean, a rapper, musician, and actor, best described the changes in hip-hop and how history just repeats itself in his 2013 song, "Hip-Hop." This theme of history repeating itself can be seen happening today. Many of the styles of hip-hop are resurfacing in visual arts, music, hairstyles, fashion and accessories. He speaks on the fact that no matter how hip-hop has evolved over the years, the culture is all the same. The same can be said about organizational change and it'sevolution, but the ultimate goal is to remain successful and thriving. Wyclef, speak to them…

[Intro:]

Refugee public, Akon, and on and on

All hands on deck

Can I go in for a minute?

Cause there's no limit to the Cash Money Hip-Hop game

[Hook 1:]

Things done changed but they stay the same

I see molly is the new cocaine

I see them rappers with them big gold chains

Remind me of the Slick Rick rings

And Rakim was the microphone fiend

And Bobby Brown was the RnB king Yeah,

now every rapper wanna bang

What happen to the days we were all in the same gang?

[Verse 1:]

Missy and Timbaland, original dubstep

And Bambaataa had our future on tape deck

Man, my daughter is seven I had to put her in check

And let her know that K.R.S.

Is more than letters in the alphabets

She's Will.I.Am'ing with her mommy

She's like: "Dad, let me teach you how to dougie"

Things done changed but they stay the same

I'm bumping Nas in the Range down memory lane

Talib, Mos Def, PE bought them lectures

My first music video Rakim, I was the extra

Run DMC ran rap, now Run's a preacher

And we all are poor righteous teachers

Krush grooving, body moving

Rhazel, Doug E. Fresh, Biz Mark had me beat boxin'

And Kim, Foxy and Eve are all warriors
Ya MC Lytes, ya not B's, y'all Queen Latifah's
Looks... pretty Nicki's in Ibiza
And every fella had a crush on Salt N Peppa
She so Naughty By Nature, Long. Live. A$AP
Written on a Wolf Gang back pack

[Hook 2:]
Things done changed but they stay the same
I see molly is the new cocaine
Yeah I see the rappers man poppin' champagne
Them Beasty Boys that Rick Rubin
And Big L was the lyrical king, and Bobby Brown was the RnB king
And we all wanted to be Russell Simmons
What happened to the day when we were all in the same gang?

[Verse 2:]
Yeah my young cousins rock Chief Keef tattoos
They say Easy E, what an attitude
I'm talking Cypress Hill, I'm talking Ice Cube
I'm talking Ice-T, Dr Dre, Snoop
Bone Thugs-n-Harmony, Crucial Conflict
Twista, Tech N9ne, flipped it this way
I'm talking from back in the day in the bay
Keak Da Sneak and the homie Mack Dre
They should have made a hip-hop dictionary written by E-40

Red & Meth, Keith Murray, Kanye, Trick Daddy, Too $hort

Flo ridin' with a Pitbull, Miami going crazy

Bambi, Pimp C, UGK, Master P

Had me listening to the south in a new way

And I miss Outkast like people miss the Fugees

And there's a Birdman watching over New Orleans

And Scarface never seen a thug cry

Till he seen his Dogg Nate singin' hooks from the sky

[Hook 3:]

Things done changed but they stay the same

I see molly is the new cocaine

I see them rappers with the big gold chains

LL Cool J Ja, Irv, Murder Inc Fat Joe, Big Pun, Cuban Link

We all wanted 5 mics in The Source magazine

French Montana at the Red Café

Wiz Khalifa roll the paper up 'we're all in the same gang'

[Verse 3:]

When I hear Waka, I hear ODB slang

I'm talking Wu-Tang, Raekwon, 2Chainz

EPMD remind me of them Coke boys

And Joey Bada$$'s, Uncle Murda, boys

Grandmaster Flash red alert, I'm talking Kool Herc

Jazzy Jeff, Fresh Prince brought it to suburbs

And hip-hop will never be the same

Since Eminem lost Proof and Heavy's out the game

We still immortal with the technique, making good music

But the tables ain't been the same since Jam Master used it

And Common used to love her and her 2Live Crew

Cause she stuck to her roots and let the DJ Screw

From Busta, Jay, Meek Mills to Tip to Quik

Kendrick Lamar, Luda, Ross, Wayne and Drake

50, Future & Game, Tribe Quest, Wale

And if we miss you, Puff Daddy do the remix

[Hook 4:]

Things done changed but they stay the same

I see molly is the new cocaine

A new Jesus piece with Chris Lighty's name

Biggy and Pac, East and West Coast kids

Mary J Blige, RnB queen

G-Unit, Ruff Ryders, Mobb Deep, DMX

Lox, Dipset, and we all in same game

Lyor Cohen

Hip-Hop

Hip-Hop

Hip-Hop

Hip-Hop

Hip-Hop Evolution

Hip-hop constantly changes and evolves on a day-to-day and like most business owners who have had to make tough decisions in order to stay current and relevant during change, one is left with the possibility of upsetting someone or as the saying goes, "stepping on someone's toes." Hip-hop mogul and Queens, New York native, Russell Simmons, constantly changed with the times in hip-hop. He was one of the major faces of Def Jam that allowed hip-hop to be brought to the masses in a straight-forward way as well as other

brands (like the brand synergy with Adidas and the creation of his own clothing line, Phat Farm) to follow after it. He stood at the center of hip-hop's growth, making sure his artists were properly exposed. He cross-marketed a youth cultural movement in music, comedy, fashion, poetry, and social action. Simmons helped form the group Run-DMC in 1983, and it wasn't until then that the music form of rap music would reach mainstream. With their authenticity and urge to stay true to themselves, Simmons pushed them to write what would be a major hit and begin hip-hop brand synergies in fashion with "My Adidas." He paired his artists to create music with other bands outside of the genre like Aerosmith, and signed the Beastie Boys, showing that hip-hop was not race-based or limited to crossover with other genres. Like all great leaders, there must be an even greater team. Russell Simmons teamed up with many people that left a major impact, like Rick Rubin with Def Jam, but also with a major player who would help in the longevity of the business of hip-hop. With that said, let's look at the man behind the scenes, Lyor Cohen.

Lyor Cohen is considered one of hip-hop's greatest pioneer executives. Like the nature of hip-hop, Cohen had to rise in the ranks of his position through hard work and dedication. With over 30-years in the music business, Cohen started his career as Russell Simmons' assistant, and worked his way up to the head of the hip-hop game. His legacy may be that of the man who brought hip-hop to a global audience: he partnered Run-DMC with Adidas, branching out from an office in SoHo to outposts in Atlanta, Los Angeles, London, Germany, and Tokyo.

Russell Simmons faced many challenges taking hip-hop culture to the mainstream. With Lyor Cohen on his team, they were able to bridge that gap with going mainstream and allowing artists and talents (employees) to get heard, (thus eliminating a form of employee silence). It can be seen as odd that Cohen would work this hard to create a gateway for the culture of hip-hop, being that his management styles are considered rather harsh and focused on benefitting self. His management strategy was often compared as a combination of Darwinism and Machiavellian. Cohen has also been linked with many different experiences from other artists or business partners, that were not portrayed as positive forms of character. However, in a cut-throat industry, these stern management tactics are needed in order to compete and thrive in the marketplace, and his résumé shows it.

Cohen was the president of Def Jam for 10 years, after working at Rush Management where he managed the careers of rap groups including Run-D.M.C., DJ Jazzy Jeff & the Fresh Prince, the Beastie Boys, Eric B and Rakim, Public Enemy, LL Cool J, and Kurtis Blow. He was president of the Island Def Jam Music Group from 1998 to 2003, after merging Island, Mercury, and Def Jam Recordings. He also served as the president and chief executive officer of Warner Music's recorded music operations, where he was responsible for all worldwide recorded music including U.S. label groups Atlantic Records and Warner Bros. Records. He is currently the CEO and co-founder of 300 Entertainment – an indie recording label that he formed in 2012.

Cohen is always expanding the views and access to hip-hop culture, and now he is focused on YouTube. Many music executives are struggling with the sale of CDs and albums thanks to online streaming, by organizing the change amongst how music or parts of hip-hop are broadcasted, it can yet again keep up with the change in societal behavior. In an interview with Complex News, Cohen stated that he feels his role as YouTube's Global

Head of Music is, "first, helping the music community embrace the technological shifts we're seeing in music today, so we can take the confusion and distrust out of the equation." This venture ideally is viewed as beneficial to artists, music executives, as well as the consumers. Cohen's vision to move towards a more collaborative relationship between the music industry and the technologies shaping the world around it.

Who is to say how much further YouTube can expand hip-hop? Cohen, with the help of others, has already expanded hip-hop on a global scale and aided in the evolution of hip-hop by bridging together different genres of music and their artists, to fashion, and much more.

CHAPTER 3

STRENGTHENING LEADERSHIP & MANAGEMENT

Now do me a favor.

Close your eyes.

Picture flashing lights

Brooklyn native Fabolous

A huge crowd chanting

BROOOOOKLYNNNN....BROOOOOKLYYNNNN

YEEEERRRRRRRRRRRRRRRRRRRR!!!! (The New York call)

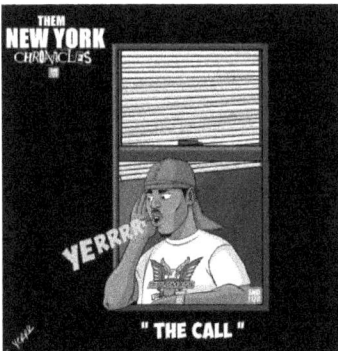

A call I say to my friends near and far, phone call or in person, to acknowledge their presence and our Brooklyn hip-hop connection. With this simple form of expression, I can express different responses to my friends that they understand without having that verbal discussion to lay down our understanding of the call. Brooklyn is known for calls as such that have changed over the time, thanks to the influences of many artists like Fabolous, Dipset, and Jay-Z to name a few.

Fabolous is a Brooklyn native and rapper who was one of the first East Coast emcees to embrace the bling mentality of the South, take on the gangsta swagger of the West Coast, as well as incorporate a subtle undercurrent of pop-rap into his music. Growing up in Brooklyn, New York, a lot of my fondest memories were in places that have long closed down like the Empire Skating Rink. Imagine a Friday night in 2006, I was finally 13-years-old and able to go to teen night with my friends at Empire. The music is bumping over the loud speakers and Fabolous' "Can't Deny It" featuring the late West Coast hip-hop pioneer, Nate Dogg, is grabbing the crowd with its beat and catchy lyrics. The crowd recites ever lyric and the roller rink is reaching its peak.

Fabolous was able to crossover in many markets of hip-hop successfully and internationally. One of my all-time favorite songs, featuring Canadian singer-songwriter Tamia, "Into You" is still one of the greatest hip-hop love songs in the 2000s. On Christmas Day, he released his *The Young OG Project* album, which housed the iconic song "Ball Drop" featuring French Montana and lead us into the year of online music streaming. It was considered the 2015 New Year anthem. In one verse, Fabolous speaks on his plans of success for the New Year and how people have taken his overall style only to boost his career as an artist and into different markets of hip-hop. He focuses on the theme "out with the old and in with the new," to only ironically represent 90s hip-hop throughout the whole *The Young OG Project*.

"This the new year resolution

We gotta be the winners cause the rest is losin'

I told 'em get money, that's the best solution

When you do, wear your rock- et like you rest in Houston

When niggas stole my style,

I ain't stress the boostin'

It's time to make more money, less excuses

My old bitch on death row, it's time for execution

My new bitch is bad ass, she the best since Boosie."

– "Ball Drop" by Fabolous ft. French Montana

The year 2015 was the year of music streaming in which Lyor Cohen explored options that would change hip-hop outside of his most recent collaboration with YouTube, in terms of business. Let's call this the year of strengthening leadership and management. Cohen originally explored options to pair hip-hop with streamlines such as Apple (founder Steve Jobs) and Spotify (founder Daniel Ek). Cohen's interest in Apple specifically was to combat the loss of sales by the artists whose music is streamed online at cheaper price points (songs being sold individually for 99 cents). Cohen and other label heads wanted the flexibility to charge more for hit songs as a way to counterbalance the lost revenue that resulted from the decoupling of full albums.

According to an article in the *New York Times*, throughout 2015, on outlets like Spotify, Rhapsody, and Apple Music, releases by hip-hop and rhythm-and-blues acts including Drake, Kendrick Lamar, ASAP Rocky, and the Weeknd consistently posted far higher numbers than artists in other genres. Streaming music is so prevalent now that is has allowed more popular acts to be streamed on different sites like Apple Music, Tidal, Spotify, while allowing new independent acts to be found on streamlines like SoundCloud. While trying to fix some underlying issues with streaming hip-hop across the Apple platform, Cohen ran into issues with Apple Genius.

Steve Jobs is one of the most influential people of my time in technology that intertwined with many platforms including my love hip-hop. Jobs' leadership style was not perfect, but it worked for him. His blunt comments, insulting words, and need for perfection gave some negative qualities to his leadership style. His pressured work environment and high demands put stress on his employees, which caused a high turnover with his team. Cohen held an interview where he spoke about his view on Steve Jobs.

"My firsthand experience with Steve [Jobs] was that he was determined and was going to get only what he wanted," he told a British newspaper. "And he was a bully. He was very seductive, but a profound bully. And oftentimes he did not say the truth." When asked if he meant Jobs was making empty promises to the music industry, Cohen responded, "Yes." Hmmm, now isn't that the pot calling the kettle black...

However, through Jobs' transforming his company, he had many followers who were loyal to him and the company, even if they weren't fully happy. Steve Jobs wore many hats in his leadership style, which is why it can be closely related to being a Situational Leadership style, as it changed based on circumstances.

His legacy lives on showing that his high demands, sometimes nasty attitude, and strive for perfection, were just the underlying qualities of a great leader who achieved one of his biggest goals, which was to be impactful.

Overview of Leadership Theories

Being a successful leader is not easy and everyone's leadership style and concepts are different, so knowing how to run an organization in each leadership style is key, especially for the one that best suits you and your business. In organizations and even in hip-hop, today the leader (industries) and teams (artists) depict how successful it can be. During my studies on leadership, I came across a common theme that is seen amongst those who are considered great leaders, they care more about the people they lead instead of themselves. There are four main theories of leadership: trait theories, behavioral theories, contingency theories, and transformational theories.

- Trait theories focus on the traits different individuals possess in order to be considered a leader. Early researchers often assumed that there is a definite set of characteristics that make a great leader, no matter the situation. If an individual did not hold these characteristics, he was not considered a great leader.

- Behavioral theories focus on the behavior leaders show in their leadership. These leadership traits are learned at an early age or over time. Early researchers started to observe what leaders did – how they behaved (especially towards followers). It later evolved from the leaders to how the overall leadership behaved, becoming the dominant way of approaching leadership within organizations in the 1950s and early 1960s.

- Contingency theories are based on the situation at hand. Each situation creates a specific mixture of factors that would create the needed leadership. Effective leadership is one that encompasses different skills that adapt to each situation.

- Transformational theories focus on the awareness and value of outcomes in the organization. They challenged the individual to analyze their individual needs and self-interests, to change them into the requirements and wants of the company, to have all employees on the same page, pushing for the same designated goal.

Breakdown of Leadership Theories & Styles

As a leader, you must be able to understand the leadership styles that work for you and your team. In terms of hip-hop, let's say you need to understand the industry and the artists. Each leadership style should be considered with factors in mind like the kind of career you have, the people you are reaching out to, and the structure of your organization. In hip-hop, you keep in mind the target market (art, fashion, music, film, etc.), the audience you are trying to reach, and how you are going to complete each process. Let's start by exploring the first of the four main theories of leadership, Trait Theory of Leadership.

Trait Theory of Leadership assumes that people are born with inherited traits and some of these traits are particularly suited to leadership. A combination of these personality traits is seen amongst people who might make great leaders or are seen as helpful in times of leading others. According to Technofunc, leading global research and consulting firm, the trait theory is quite complex and there is bound to be subjective judgment in determining who is regarded as a 'good' or 'successful' leader and many of these factors are situational related factors. Although some people are born leaders, some have manifested into their leadership roles due to certain circumstances. In hip-hop, successful leaders have different traits that lead to success. For example, Sean "P. Diddy" Combs from Bad Boy Records, has the openness trait in his leadership style, while Suge Knight from Death Row Records, has the neuroticism trait, even though his actions cost him to lose everything.

In the trait theory, the focus is solely on the leader of the organization and not on those who are under them or the situation at hand. The trait approach suggests that organizations will work better if the people in managerial positions have specific leadership profiles. This theory helps leaders or individuals become aware of themselves and aides them in development as an individual but also as a member of a team. By analyzing their own traits, managers can gain an idea of their strengths and weaknesses. A trait assessment can help managers determine whether they have the qualities to move up or to move to other positions in the company.

If the trait theory of leadership is one you would consider implement in the workplace, then it is imperative as a leader to be very aware of yourself and the traits and values you bring to your team. To be a successful leader you should use the Big 5 Personality traits as a base to narrow down the traits that would benefit the field you are in. Based on the strongest traits that each member possesses, a great leader will place their employees in the area of the organization where they can excel. A successful leader will personally get to know staff members they are working with, so they can understand each individual's traits. Try to find out the goals each staff member would like to reach and support them by focusing on their strengths and aide them with their weaknesses. Individuals can be assessed and can get an in-depth understanding of their identity and the way they will affect others in the organization. This can be translated into different forms of teamwork. Teamwork is crucial in any organization, and how each member and the team can affect the production of the company. Team building exercises and different training opportunities should be made available to staff. These activities can support staff in achieving their personal goals as well as the goals of the organization.

Mic Check 1..2..1..2

Hip-hop emerged in 1978, even though elements of hip-hop were prevalent in the early 1970s. According to disc jockey, singer, songwriter, and producer, Afrika Bambaataa, the elements that make hip-hop are the Big 4: DJing (aural), MCing (aural), Aerosol Writing (visual), and B-boying (physical). Doug E. Fresh added Beat Boxing (aural) making it the fifth element. However, KRS-One includes Beat Boxing in DJing, keeping the number of elements at four.

Leaders who are focused on improving the future, follow the Transformational Leadership style. Transformational leaders are focused on making tomorrow better. They do so in four steps: vision, authenticity, growth mindset, and creativity. Transformational leaders work towards a noble vision, act with authenticity and honesty, adopt a growth mindset, and promote creativity and new ideas. According to a study on Transactional, Transformational, and Transcendent Leadership conducted by John Jacob Gardiner, a Professor of Leadership at Seattle University, transformational leadership, "is a relationship of mutual stimulation and elevation that converts followers into leaders and may convert leaders into moral agents." Transformational leaders try to combine the goals of the employee with the goals of the organization to promote growth amongst both the employee and the organization.

If you are in a field that might deal with children or young adults, transformational leadership might be a good leadership style to implement. In order to be successful at being a trans-formational leader, you should delegate the roles and duties of each team member and provide them with expectations that they must uphold. Try to mix the goals of each individual team member with that of the goals of the organization. Also, observe your team members and provide feedback and support when needed, so they are always learning and improving themselves. Finally, never be too afraid to acknowledge the accomplishments of your team members whether big or small. It will inspire them to continue to improve and succeed in their career.

"I'm not a businessman, I'm a Business, man." _Jay-Z

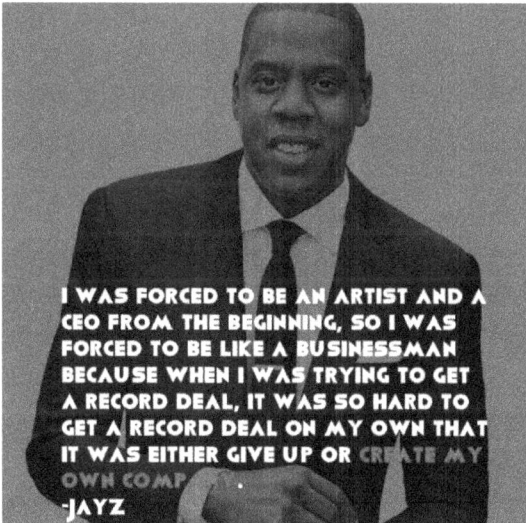

I WAS FORCED TO BE AN ARTIST AND A CEO FROM THE BEGINNING, SO I WAS FORCED TO BE LIKE A BUSINESSMAN BECAUSE WHEN I WAS TRYING TO GET A RECORD DEAL, IT WAS SO HARD TO GET A RECORD DEAL ON MY OWN THAT IT WAS EITHER GIVE UP OR CREATE MY OWN COMPANY.
-JAYZ

This iconic line from Jay-Z's verse to Kanye West's "Dia-monds from Sierra Leone" Remix, captivated the minds of many hip-hop lovers. As discussed in chapter one, Jay-Z is a transformational leader who transformed others into leaders as well. Many of his songs speak to how anyone can make it to the level of success he did. In his recent project 4:44, Jay-Z uses clever wordplay in his song "The Story of O.J." to correlate between price and actual worth, where he offers his album for a price that doesn't match its worth, the costs to stream on his online company, Tidal. Clever.

> *"But I'm tryin' to give you a million dollars' worth of game for $9.99."*
>
> _Jay Z

On the other hand of transformational leadership, there is the Transactional Leadership style. This style runs under the premise of actions and reactions. It uses a sequence of transactions where the actions of employees result in either a reward or punishment. Transactional leadership promotes a motivation in employees to work harder towards organizational goals because they will achieve something that will benefit them. This leadership style also promotes accountability and self-awareness in employees and can be seen in organizations that have hierarchical structured management.

In order to be a successful leader using the transactional leadership style, you should develop an appropriate hierarchy structure that can benefit both you and your team. You should open the lines for communication so that members at the lower end of the structure can feel just as involved or valued as leadership members. You should also come up with incentives to benefit your team members individually and as a team. These incentives should be a mixture of both short-term and long-term benefits that their motivation to work to the best of their ability does not fall short.

"Try to be the king, but the ace is back." _Dr. Dre

Rapper, record producer, and entrepreneur, Dr. Dre, is a prime example of a transactional leader and business manager. His focus on brand identity to reach his audience is the key to his success. Dr. Dre first started his career with the notorious rap group N.W.A. and masterminded their 1989 breakthrough album *Straight Outta Compton*. He later branched into co-founding Death Row Records until his departure in 1996. He then founded Aftermath Entertainment and Beats by Dre, and partnered with music icon and record producer, Jimmy Iovine. Dr. Dre started with Beats Music, an online streaming services, which lead to his headphone brand Beats by Dre, that later was acquired by Apple in a billion-dollar deal. This deal was by far one of the most expensive deals in Apple history, making Dr. Dre the first rapper to become a billionaire. His love for music expanded to develop a different brand that increased his transactions not just amongst other artists, but amongst all age groups worldwide. Dr. Dre expanded his reach from CD to streaming sales with the use of his Beats Music services and took it over the top by using his headphones to move into a bigger technological/fashion field. Before Beats By Dre, headphones costing over $100 rarely sold well, but since its 2008 launch when it was promoted mainly to a youth-oriented market, kids lined up to buy a pair (with some models reaching a price tag of $300). His headphones main basis was no longer only focused on the music, but it became a fashion statement merging many business platforms.

Often leaders are faced with different situations that occur and there is no specific leadership style that would best suit it. Situational Leadership is based on how people react to being a part of a team during a given situation. Paul Hersey, the founder and CEO of the Center of Leadership Studies based situational leadership on an interplay among (1) the amount of direction a leader gives (task behavior), (2) the amount of socio-emotional support a leader provides (relationship behavior), and (3) the "readiness" level that followers exhibit on a specific task, function, activity, or objective that the leader is attempting to accomplish through the individual or group. This leadership theory holds four different leadership styles. Directing (S1) is used for employees who have low competence but have a high commitment to the task at hand. The leader uses high directive behavior and low supportive behavior. Coaching (S2) is used for employees with some competence and some commitment to the task, where the leader would use high supportive and directive behavior. Supporting (S3) is used for employees with high competence and variable commitment of the task. The leader uses high supportive behavior and low directive behavior. Finally, delegating (S4) is used for employees with both high levels of competence and commitment to the task. The leader uses low supportive and directive behavior. When employees hold a level of maturity and readiness, the need for leader support and structure decreases. An employee's level of readiness is based on their knowledge, skills, and experiences. If employees are at different stages of maturity and readiness, the leader must depict what they see suitable for the supervision of each individual employee. This calls for the leader to have the ability to adapt to the changes and the situation they are dealing with as well as the type of employee they are managing. Often in the hip-hop community, managers of artists go through different phases to help the artist develop over time. The manager must use the situation of their artist (whether it is good public presence or bad public presence) as the basis of how they will help move along and/or influence their career.

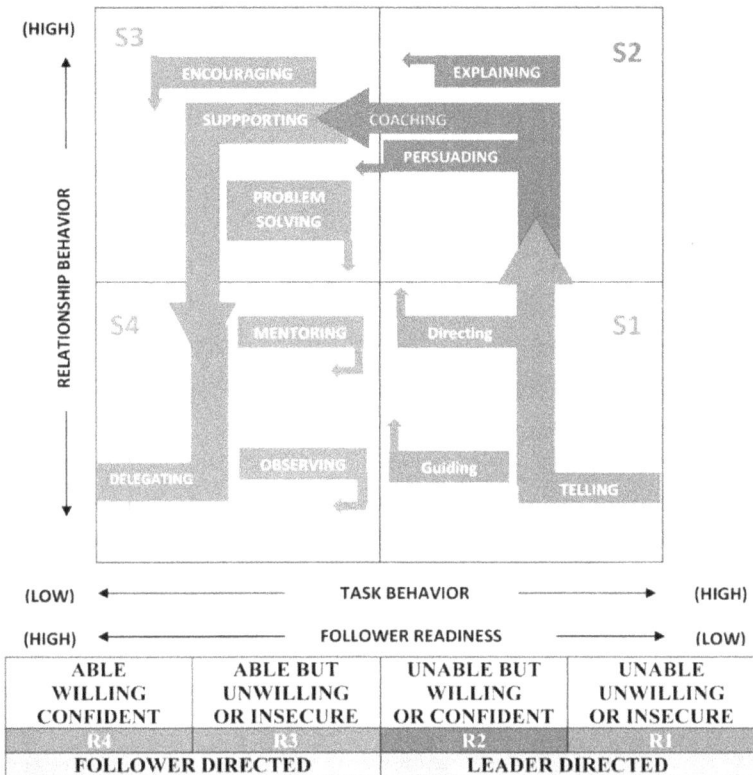

ABLE WILLING CONFIDENT	ABLE BUT UNWILLING OR INSECURE	UNABLE BUT WILLING OR CONFIDENT	UNABLE UNWILLING OR INSECURE
R4	R3	R2	R1
FOLLOWER DIRECTED		LEADER DIRECTED	

To be a successful leader using the situational leadership theory, I believe all factors should be taken into consideration. Develop how to approach each team member with their unique level of.maturity and readiness to work. Combine goals with that of similar interest or skill. If you are dealing with a team member who is very committed but lacks understanding or skill of the task, provide them with a more directing leadership style. If you are dealing with a member who has some knowledge of the task and some commitment to further learning it, provide a coaching role. If you are dealing with a member who has a high understanding of the task, however their commitment varies, provide a support role. This way the member can feel free to explore the task on their own. Finally, if you are dealing with members who are both highly knowledgeable of the task and committed to learning and doing more, delegate them duties so they can implement what they know. Placing them in a smaller leading role can also be beneficial because it can help them assist fellow team members but also give them a greater sense of responsibility and accountability.

Hip-hop changes based on the situation or the times at hand; many artists use what is going on in society or in their personal lives to fuel their creativity. In this case, when working with artists or even encountering them, having a situational leadership style is beneficial. TLC, the biggest R&B, pop, and commercial female rap group in history can attest to this. Tionne "T-Boz" Watkins, Lisa "Left Eye" Lopes, and Rozonda "Chilli" Thomas, were the iconic lineup for the American female group that was formed in Atlanta, Georgia in 1990. They were led by the leadership of Perri "Pebbles" Reid and her company Pebbitone, where they rose to become the biggest and top-selling group of all time, with some bumps along the

road. With all three members producing a different sound and style of music (T-Boz's blend of funk, Left Eye's blend of hip-hop, and Chilli's blend of R&B), Pebbles had to have a situational leadership style to create a solid group that highlighted each talent both individually and as a unit. Each group member also dealt with their own separate situations in their personal lives, but that did not stop them from delivering an amazing musical legacy.

In a sense, a good leader is serving their team members by adapting to aide each member in their own unique way. Each member of the team is different, with unique skill sets and personality traits. A great leader can bring out the best in their team members. In a servant leadership, the leader is more focused on the needs and desires of others. This style of leadership was first proposed by Robert K. Greenleaf in 1970, and it supports a leader's main motivation and role service to others. They focus on four central ideas: service to others, holistic approach, promoting a sense of community, and sharing of power in decision-making.

Service to others means to encourage greatness from your team while the organizational success is indirect. A holistic approach to work focuses on people being who they are in their professional and personal lives, which benefits the interests and performance of the organization. Promoting a sense of community, encourages the need for communities, for the organization to succeed. Employees working together as a unit provides a service to those around them, not the institution alone. Sharing of power in decision-making is best utilized in this leadership environment because it promotes participatory, empowering environments, and encourages the talents of followers. The servant-leader creates a more effective, motivated workforce and ultimately a more successful organization. Just like any trait that can be seen in leaders and team members, the servant leadership is seen to have ten personal characteristics: listening, empathy, healing, awareness, persuasion, conceptualization, foresight, stewardship, commitment to the growth of people, and building a community. A servant leader enables growth and inspires others to grow and possibly exceed greatness. Servant leaders serve others through their actions.

"My music is so much bigger than me, and what I am." – Pharrell

Pharrell Williams is a rapper, singer, songwriter, and record producer from Virginia Beach, Virginia. He is best known for his record production duo with Chad Hugo, The Neptunes, and also as the lead vocalist of the band N*E*R*D. Pharrell has made a name for himself with his many productions and collaborations with many amazing artists like Snoop Dogg, Jay-Z, Lil' Kim, Ludacris, and much more. He is an example of servant leadership in that he used his artistic skills to display to the hip-hop community around him. In 2014, he contributed a song called "Happy" to the *Despicable Me 2* soundtrack and released it as a single. This melodic song brought happiness and joy around the globe with its funk/neo-soul vibe, and ultimately struck gold for the hip-hop icon. This single gained worldwide recognition and created a chain reaction of videos from different people all over the world expressing their love for the hit single. In order to promote the single release, Pharell launched the website 24hoursofhappy.com, to visually display a 24-hour loop of "Happy" showing various people in Los Angeles, California dancing and enjoying the song. Many different celebrities, as well as Pharrell himself, and the Despicable Me characters make appearances in the first 24-hour music video. This video alone sparked a worldwide phenomenon, as many people from cities around the world would recreate their own "Happy" video and post them on the internet to be seen by the masses. "Happy" reached triple platinum, is the fourth single to achieve such a goal in the past 20 years. It also won the Grammy Award for Best Music Video and is the most successful song of 2014 with millions of sales and streams worldwide.

In order to be a successful servant leader, you should promote the four central ideas. Encourage your staff to be great and to work on their goals as individuals; improving themselves produces positive results for the organization. Encourage and embrace individuality and uniqueness. As a leader, you can provide weekly showcases or acknowledgments on small personal goals giving each member the opportunity to better themselves. Promote a sense of community by providing small daily team building activities so that each member can interact with their fellow team members and improve team culture. Finally, provide weekly meetings and social gatherings that allow team members time to brainstorm new ideas and solutions to problems that can change their community in a positive and effective way.

In another form of leadership, there is Maxwell's 360 Degree Leadership style. John Maxwell is a world-renowned author, speaker, and pastor, whose primary focus is on leadership. He devised the 360 Degree Leadership style to focus on three levels of leadership: up, across, and down.

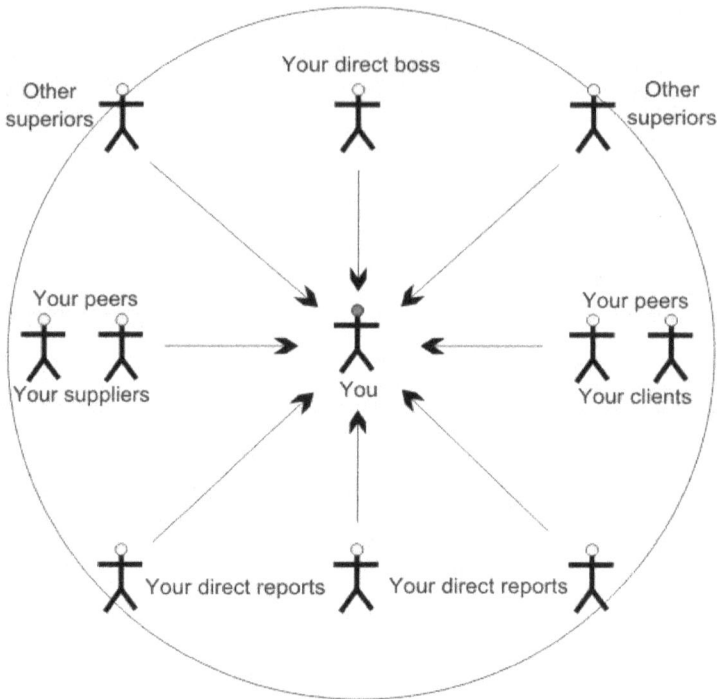

The leading up principle focuses on how to influence those above you in the organization. Influencing the leaders in your organization include being a leader of your own and bringing value to your leadership member by being a reliable and supportive member of the team. There are nine principles in the lead up leadership:

1. Lead yourself exceptionally well
2. Lighten your leader's load
3. Be willing to do what others won't
4. Do more than managing. Lead!
5. Invest in relational chemistry.
6. Be prepared every time you take your leader's time.
7. Know when to push and when to back off.
8. Become a go-to player.
9. Be better tomorrow than you are today.

Leading across deals with how you influence your peers. In this exchange, Maxwell stressed that it could be very difficult (particularly if one is doing well at leading up, which may lead to suspicion or jealousy from one's peers). Influencing your fellow peers, involves growing relationships within the company and allowing others to show their talents and contributions to the team. There are seven principles in the lead across leadership:

1. Understand, practice, and complete the leadership loop.
2. Put completing fellow ahead of competing with them.
3. Be a friend.
4. Avoid office politics.
5. Expand your circle of acquaintances.
6. Let the best idea win.
7. Don't pretend you're perfect.

Finally, leading down deals with how leaders add value to people that are following them. Good leaders are committed to helping those who are following them. There are seven principles in the lead down leadership:

1. Walk slowly through the halls.
2. See everyone as a "10".
3. Develop each team member as a person.
4. Place people in their strength zones.
5. Model the behavior you desire.
6. Transfer the vision.
7. Reward for results.

Using Maxwell's 360 Degree Leadership strategies, on doing so based on the up, across, and down levels of leadership. In leading up, focus on influencing upper management. Implement the principle of "Do more than manage. Lead!" Take the initiative and assist other leadership groups. Guide your fellow colleagues in completing work and aid in different areas. This will take you into leading across and influencing your peers positively. Influencing your peers involves growing relationships within the company and allowing others to show their talents and contributions to the team. Implement the principle of expanding your acquaintances. Networking within an organization is crucial, as it opens the opportunity to meet individuals who can help shape your career or enhance your skills over time. Finally, by leading downwards and following the principle of developing each team member as a person, not only develops the skills of the leader by allowing them to develop the skills of other team members but is also shows your investment in their success within the organization.

A good leader should also know the strengths and weaknesses of their team members. In this leadership style, the focus is on how to use strengths in organizations to excel. This style is called Strength-Based Leadership. According to the study, "Strengths Coaching With Leaders," conducted by Alex Linley, Linda Woolston, and Robert Biswas-Diener in 2009, found that when people used their strengths, they were happier and fulfilled, achieved their goals more effectively, and are more engaged to perform better at work. The researchers summarize that, "it is for all of these reasons that we promote strengths coaching as an effective, value adding organizational intervention." Strength-based leadership focuses on positivity and employees working on their strengths to provide a better more productive work experience. There are four notable domains of leadership strength: executing, influencing, relationship building, and strategic thinking.

To be successful in the strength-based leadership style, you should pay close attention to the use of your strengths within the workplace. Also, manage emotions and behaviors in the workplace that promote professionalism and respect. When dealing with any situation in the workplace it is best to stay calm and handle each situation to the best of your ability. You should focus on not overusing your strengths especially when they are not needed or can be used against you. Strengths can become weaknesses especially when there is no balance or too much of it. For instance, people can be caring leaders which can benefit their employees. However, if they become too caring, they can be viewed as a feeble leader. Do not apply strengths during in-appropriate times. This is called lopsided leadership where the leader is focused on applying a strength that is not applicable to a situation and does not focus on the underlying strength that is needed. When these two things happen, it can have an adverse negative effect on the team and the organization. Focus tasks on the strengths of your teams and provide guidelines on how not to overuse your strengths. Also, offer opportunities to give and receive feedback. Often leaders do not know that they are lopsided, when there is trust amongst the team and their leader, this form of communication can be the strongest.

In terms of hip-hop in the music industry, this can be seen in how music executives push their artists. Music executives pro-mote and push their artists' brands, as well as create the connec-tions for other labels and outside markets. In hip-hop, one of the most prominent music executives that has transformed himself over the years is none other than DJ Khaled.

We The Best!

DJ Khaled is a record producer, radio personality, DJ, record label executive, and author. He has made many chart-topping hits that are my all-time favorites, with artists like Rihanna, Drake, Bryson Tiller, Future, Justin Bieber and many more. He is also an avid sneaker enthusiast like myself, owning many pairs of rare or unreleased sneakers like Air Jordans. Later, I will discuss hip-hop's influence on sports and apparel. His career started off rocky, as he was homeless pursuing his dreams. He was a child of immigrant parents and worked his way up from Djing school dances in Orlando, Florida to be at the top of the music scene in Miami. He was the DJ for the hip-hop group Terror Squad, assisted and produced many hit singles and records, and has made cameo appearances for promotional material and movies like *Shottas*, *Pitch Perfect 3*, and *Spider-Man: Homecoming*. Now he is one of the most influential artists in hip-hop and on the Snapchat platform. With his extremely large personality, DJ Khaled became an internet phenomenon by turning this small social media platform into his personal entries promoting health, sermons on success, and just everyday fun with his family and his career.

Leadership Management

In leadership management, two minds have left a major impact on the world, Warren Bennis and Peter Drucker. Warren Bennis (born March 8th, 1925) was a scholar, organizational consultant and author, from New York City who was widely considered the originator of the contemporary field of Leadership Studies. Peter Drucker (born November 19th, 1909) was a management consultant, educator, and author whose writings contributed to the practical and philosophical foundations for a modern business corporation. Both individuals had similar yet different approaches to leadership. Bennis looked at three situations in which leaders are formed – Learning from Difference, Prevailing Over Darkness, and Meeting Great Expectation. He believed these skills are developed in different periods of life due to the circumstances experienced. This can be seen similar to situational leadership. In hip-hop, many artists have gone through one of the three situations in which they became the leader and artist they are today. Some artists have even experienced more than others and have had a combination of all three types of life situations take place, causing them to evolve, acquire, and possess the four skills that Bennis noted great leaders hold: the ability to engage others in a shared meaning, distinctive and compelling voice, possess integrity and a strong set of values, with an adaptive capacity. In 2007, Bennis also stated that great leaders have six competencies:

- Create a sense of mission
- Motivate others
- Create an adaptive social architecture
- Generate trust and optimism
- Develop other leaders
- Get results

Bennis believed that adaptive capacity is the most crucial skill to have in order to be a great leader. His focus was more so on the leader adapting to the changes or improving over time through different situations, instead of just excelling in his area of expertise. In this case, the leader can be seen to take on multiple hats to get the job done instead of allowing a team member to excel in an area he isn't strong in.

Drucker was focused on the purpose the leader had in the organization. He believed that all leaders serve a purpose by having a goal or vision, and showing it to their organization. They place team members in areas they know they will succeed in. Drucker viewed the corporation as human cooperation. He stated that, "skills can be acquired, not values. Those who are unhappy are seen in positions where the values of the organization don't fit them." In a 2004 article in *Forbes* magazine, publisher and entrepreneur Rich Karlgaardrecalled his conversation with Peter Drucker on leadership. Drucker's thoughts on leadership are as follows:

- Make sure the necessities get done, even if a team member completes it
- Check performance
- Mission-driven
- Practice creative abandonment

Drucker focused on what was needed to be done, the skills needed to be a great leader, and the actions that followed behind it by the team. He focused on the skills of the team and how they benefit and compliment the leader.

Following the leadership style of Bennis, you need to create a mission where all team members are aware of the common goal. Be motivational and supportive. Develop other team members to become leaders. Gain trust and optimism amongst your team members. Open the lines of communication on all levels of leadership. Have a confident, distinctive, and compelling voice that will capture the attention of your team members. Have a strong set of values so that your team members know what is expected of them.

Following the leadership style of Drucker, focus on what your goal is and communicate that with your organization. Be mission-driven and make sure the goals are attainable and realistic. Place members in areas they will succeed in. Consistently check the performance of your team and yourself so that you are aware of anything that can be causing a negative effect on the company and can adjust it in a timely fashion as not to create much damage. Practice creative abandonment and know when to put more energy into another goal once the original goal is accomplished and is stable. If you remove the support and resources too soon, it can potentially cause a major setback. Allow others to show their value or expertise in the time of need. Good leaders encourage all team members to showcase their strengths because all are valuable members within the organization.

In conclusion, how to become a successful leader in any leadership style starts with you. A successful leader must care for their followers, be a good listener, be supportive, and motivational to their teams. All leadership theories have common rules that will aid in the success of a leader. These rules are:

- Develop a mission
- Communication is key
- Place members in the areas they are strongest in
- Create expectations

- Team building activities
- Motivate your team members
- Generate trust
- Provide support
- Allow feedback to be given and received

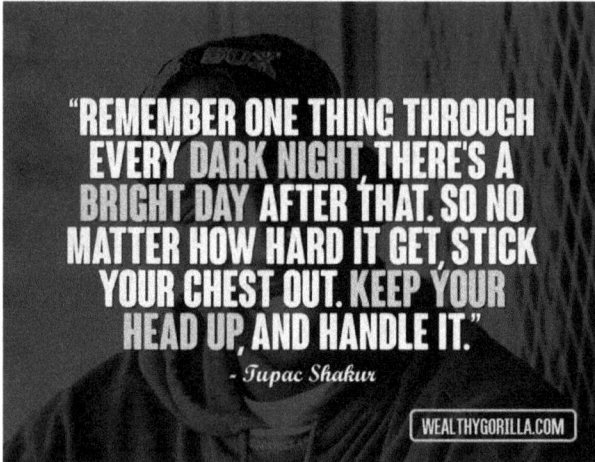

"REMEMBER ONE THING THROUGH EVERY DARK NIGHT, THERE'S A BRIGHT DAY AFTER THAT. SO NO MATTER HOW HARD IT GET, STICK YOUR CHEST OUT. KEEP YOUR HEAD UP, AND HANDLE IT."

- Tupac Shakur

WEALTHYGORILLA.COM

Strengthening "Unconventional" Hip-Hop Leadership & Management

Reaching the masses is one of an artist's main goals in hip-hop. Steve Jobs is yet again one extension of hip-hop as he has crossed the paths of many influential icons. His technological innovations allowed different outlets to merge across his Apple platform. Jobs had made an impact on other businessmen such as Lyor Cohen and Dr. Dre. Steve Jobs and Apple have had a different approach to the technological aspects of hip-hop culture.

However, all great things come with a price, right?

UNCONVENTIONAL

"Steve Jobs was an unconventional leader. His management style wasn't the stuff of university textbooks - he wasn't known for his consultative or consensus building approach." This opening statement to writer Sarah McInerney's 2011 article, "Steve

Jobs: An Unconventional Leader," was one that best described a leader who typically steps out of the normal comfort zone. In order to have had such great success, Steve Jobs was an unconventional leader who portrayed many different leadership styles but more so within the Transformational Leadership style. Jobs' leadership style (not to mention his genius) is widely seen as a key ingredient in Apple's success. Had he used a different style, he might not have achieved the same spectacular results at Apple, or even laid the proper foundation for them to excel after his departure. Apple has grown to become the world's largest information technology company and top brand items in the marketplace. Apple is noted for their $3 billion-dollar pairing with Dr. Dre's Beats Headphones in 2014, which took hip-hop to greater heights.

Transformational leaders work towards a noble vision, act with authenticity and honesty, adopt a growth mindset, and promote creativity and new ideas amongst their organization and staff members. He focused on transforming his company and his employees to reflect the organization's goals. He also favored a mixture of Situational Trait and Transactional Leadership styles. Like all great leaders, he had positive and negative leadership traits that affected his employees in different ways. However, he was a visionary who wanted to help others see the world of technology through his perspective. He created big goals for himself, his staff, and his organization to leave an important mark on the world. Steve Jobs used his platform to break down his products, so others could see creations, and how they can better influence behaviors in the future. He was able to conform to the demands of society and work with the obstacles faced in his way with his situational leadership style, and ability to adapt and adjust.

UNCONVENTIONAL

Do not forget that word, it's very important.

That one triumph with Beats took a bigger leap with Apple Music. Beats by Dre had a subscription-based online music streaming platform, Beats Music, that was also acquired during their $3 billion-dollar deal. The platform was discontinued, and the subscriptions were transferred over to the platform of Apple Music which launched in 2015. This service offers online streaming of the latest music and music videos across the board for only $9.99 a month. Unfortunately, some of my preferred choices are not available like Jay-Z (only Jay-Z carries Jay-Z music, TIDAL), Aaliyah, Beyoncé (duh she is the Queen to Jay-Z's King), and so on. This was due to many issues amongst artists and labels, and with streaming releases of their music affecting their royalty rates and sound quality, Tidal was created and launched in 2014 and disrupted the Beats platform. Tidal claims to pay the highest percentage of royalties to music artists and songwriters. This trend seems very familiar, doesn't it? Every year a new phone, every year a new product. One big deal to the next. With this cut throat, go-getter business strategy, of course another strong-minded visionary like Cohen would call Jobs a "bully."

Many critics have stated Job's leadership style should not be imitated because it may not work for everyone. Despite his unfavorable leadership style, he held characteristics of caring for his employees, inspiring and empowering those around him, and had a clear vision for his organization. The authors of the Steve Jobs biography *Becoming Steve Jobs*, Brent SchleSnder and Rick Tetzeli, described Jobs' management style as very much in sticking to who he was as a person. That should probably be the first thing a leader asks himself/herself – am I posing, or is this really me? If the answer is posing, it's time to find a new style of management.

Unfortunately, we lost this great mind in 2011 due to pancreatic cancer, but that did not stop his legacy from living on. Apple is still growing and thriving every day.

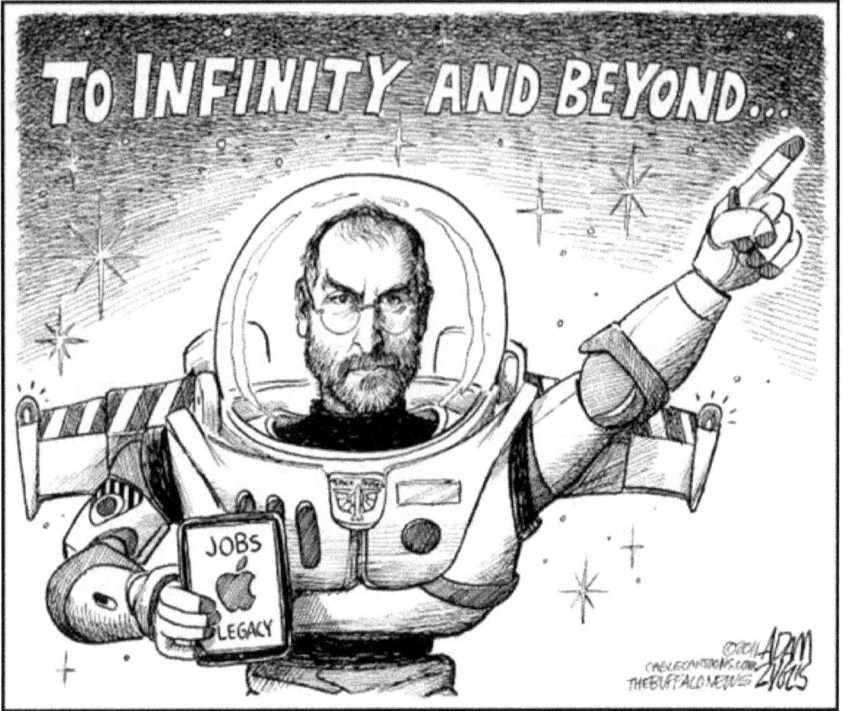

Steve Jobs lived by his words: "I want to put a ding in the universe."

CHAPTER 4

DEVELOPING HIGH-PERFORMANCE TEAMWORK

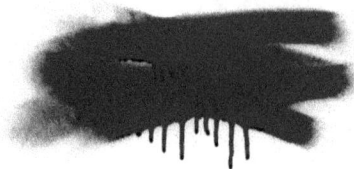

Let's go back to the year 'Greats' were created... 1993

My grand debut took place on an early spring morning, at 3:03 am when I sent my mother into labor with her third child. Fortunate enough, I didn't waste much time. Within two hours, I was flying out of her birth canal as my father strolled in from parking the car like he had time to kill. To their surprise, this bouncing baby was not the boy they anticipated but instead, the first and only girl who took her father's heart from day one. Sorry Ma, you were no longer the only lady in the house.

Aside from me busting on the scene, hip-hop's most influential group came into their own originating only twenty minutes away from me on Staten Island, NY.

WU-TANG CLAN

According to the Wu-Tang Corp official website, Wu-Tang Clan proved to be the most revolutionary rap group of the mid-90s – and only partially because of their music.

Wu-Tang Clan comprised of nine MCs who all went on to contribute to the hip-hop industry in various markets like movies, production, apparel, technology, video games, and more. RZA, Method Man, U-God, Raekwon, Ol' Dirty Bastard, Masta Killa, Inspectah Deck, GZA, and Ghostface, all took hip-hop by storm. They made a pact to form an artistic and financial community, exceeding far past just a group but becoming its own industry. We can call them the Ultimate Team of Hip-Hop. These members set a tone with the release of their debut album *Enter the Wu-Tang 36 Chambers*. They established themselves through a group effort and then would branch out into solo projects, collaborating with outside artists along the way. This allowed them to become more influential and stronger in the hip-hop community.

Like Wu-Tang's goal to be its own industry and in organizations around the world, teams are created to carry out the functions of the company and produce a successful product. For these teams to be successful, the organization and the leaders must create teams to work together to complete the tasks of the company. Each team production goes through a series of steps in order to build a well-connected team. In order to create a successful effective team, you must first start with the individuals you select on your team.

Team Members

The characteristics of individual team members influence the collective behavior of the team. The ideal characteristics of an individual that is a part of a successful team are: open-minded, can look at things from multiple points of view, and can control their polarized thinking and emotions.

An open-minded person / looking at things from multiple points of view: Team members who are open to and accepting of the viewpoints from others are more likely to actively listen to and try to understand other team members. If individuals only look at things from their point of view without seeing it from another perspective, it can cause problems. When interacting with other people around us in the workplace, this closed-minded approach can often lead to very dysfunctional behaviors, such as defensiveness, turf protection, interpersonal conflict, gossip, finger-pointing, damaging gossip—all of which destroy productive relationships.

Control polarized thinking and emotions: Polarized thinking means you swing all the way out to one end of a two-sided continuum—magnifying a situation way out of proportion and exaggerating what is happening far beyond what is actually happening. An ideal team member wouldn't make a big deal out of small situations, they would try to solve the problem at hand. Having polarized thinking can affect the team and the individual allowing help, or blaming someone else for the problems, it also affects communication amongst team members.

Most characteristics either follow or form after the characteristics of open-mindedness and the ability to control polarized thinking, due to working with others is about controlling emotions and thinking in a specific setting, as well as inviting the opinions and thoughts of others willingly instead of fighting against them. Most characteristics of individuals are emotionally and mentally based before their behavior and physical actions take place.

Team Formation

The next step would be informing the new team. The Wu-Tang Clan is an example of an unconventional hip-hop team. (Remember that word, right?) They turned the standard concept of a hip-hop crew and assembled what can be seen as a kind of support group which was comprised of nine MCs. Each member contributed to the group's efforts individually and together in order to create the dynasty they planned.

The first five steps to form a new team should be:

Mutual Vision: Without having a goal or vision to achieve, the work by the team would have no purpose. In understanding the mutual vision and trying to obtain it, the team can begin formation around a specific purpose. Find what can be called alignment amongst your team, where a group is functioning together instead of its individual members working at cross-purposes.

Open the lines of Communication: In order to fully gain supporters and ideas for the mission, you must open the lines of communication amongst your team, both good and bad. The more information employees have, the more they will feel they are a part of the organizational team.

Implement Trust: All members of your team must gain a sense of trust amongst each other. People in a group tend to feel safe when they know they won't be ridiculed, embarrassed, controlled, manipulated, exploited, or punished in any way by other group members. Implement team building activities, so they can all see the attributeseach individual can contribute to the team and vision.

Combine the values of team members with those of the organization: You must be able to combine and compliment the individual goals and values of each team member with the goals and values of the organization. A team working together to achieve an organizational mission can more effectively achieve that mission than each team member working on his or her own.

Promote self-awareness and accountability, and problem-solving skills: Allow your team members to express their ideas on how to solve the problems at hand. This will boost confidence and allow each member to be aware of their strengths and weaknesses. It will also push them to want to improve themselves and have a sense of accountability for their actions on the team. Teams are far more effective when everyone feels empowered to lead with his or her own unique expertise.

Team Leadership

In all good teams, there are leaders that guide and set the tone for their fellow counterparts. RZA was mainly accountable for the vision of the Wu-Tang Clan. With his direction, productions, and co-productions, the group and in their solo projects were able to create a hazy, surreal, and menacing soundscape out of hardcore beats, eerie piano riffs, and minimal samples. Over these tracks, each artist their unique talents, updating the old-school hip-hop attack with vicious violence, martial arts imagery, and a welcomed warped sense of humor. The sound of the Wu-Tang Clan developed was one of the most recognizable sounds in hip-hop by 1995.

Many leadership characteristics overlap, however, there are multiple characteristics you should implement. As a team leader, you should focus on the following leadership characteristics:

Mutual Trust: Trust must be present among all staff members and leaders. You all are working toward the same goal and every member should respect the work and goal of each other. Great managers should always focus on creating a code of honor for their team before they get started.

Open Communication: Again, you should promote open communication so that staff can have a voice in decision making, ideas, and problem-solving. They should be able to come to you with questions and concerns, so that there is no confusion on the expectations. It is an excellent and effective way to lay rules that everybody in the team must follow.

Empowerment and Encouragement: Encourage staff to improve themselves and work toward the goals they want to achieve. Show full support in everything that they do and provide feedback. You should also acknowledge the work that is done and acknowledge changes that can be made to help.

Team Dynamics

Next, work on team communication etiquette and team dynamic. When building your team, make sure that the team dynamics eliminate any negative effects where members can fall victim to groupthink or group conformity. Communicate without sending an underlying message. You can do team building exercises to work on communication skills. Each team member could be placed in small groups of two where they can praise and critique their partner, creating the opportunity to learn how to express themselves and learn about the effect of tone and delivery perceptions. Use each form of communication and situation as a learning experience. Learn new skills and acquire more knowledge as you go through every experience. Communicate with team members without fear of ridicule, embarrassment, or punishment. Often in teams, it is seen that conformity is present. Solomon Asch, a gestalt psychologist and pioneer in social psychology, conducted conformity experiments where he found that many people conformed due to fear of ridicule. The results also suggested that, "conformity can be influenced both by a need to fit in and a belief that other people are smarter or better informed." Be mindful of the words you use, the body language you show, and the tone in which the message is delivered. Also, challenge the minds of your team members, and acknowledge their viewpoints.

Team Processes

On the other hand, every team goes through different processes especially during a conflict or issue. The Wu-Tang Clan kept their eyes on the objective of their vision. After individually creating a name for themselves through their own individual ventures, they later reconnected to complete their second group album, all while putting the next phase of their plan in motion. The next phase consisted of unearthing new associates and spinning the resulting stable of talent into a brand-name franchise.

Conflicts arise in a workplace due to the various ideas and opinions that each unique individual brings to their team. In the case of the Wu-Tang Clan, Ol' Dirty Bastard (ODB) caused controversy amongst the group and others in the hip-hop community. He was arrested many times for different crimes like assault, robbery, failure to pay child support, and much more. He was shot in the abdomen over an argument that transpired between him and another rapper, was incarcerated several times, and even escaped his court-mandated drug facility, where he was on the run and considered a fugitive for a month. His constant legal problems and erratic behavior was only the tip of the iceberg, as it began to cause a lot of communication issues amongst the group because of the ridicule he was receiving. The Wu-Tang Clan released their second individual projects during this same period and struggled with commercial recognition due to this. It was later seen in the released FBI files of ODB that his erratic behavior also drew attention to the Wu-Tang Clan in relation to them being a criminal organization. According to Dr. Arnie Dahlke, an organizational psychologist, author, and my well-respected graduate professor, "The key to conflict resolution is to handle conflicts without you or the conflicting parties being clouded by anger, without being determined to find someone to blame and punish, and without being biased by grudges one may hold." In the case of the Wu-Tang Clan, a group intervention for ODB probably could have helped his downward spiral but also help other members of the group express concerns and look for different solutions to change the narrative of their group and ODB. A strategy on how to reduce conflict in teams, is by playing the role of facilitator or have an outside, trained neutral party act as the facilitator. Facilitators guide the group in completing the work.

Guidelines for reducing conflict:

- Attack the problem at hand not the people you are discussing it with
- Gather facts
- Assist in active listening
- Ask for suggestions on how to solve the problem at hand
- Be aware of emotions, thoughts, and body language
- Respect the other party

When conflicts arise, you should separate both parties and have one-on-one conversations to find details about the events that took place. Look for common parts of their stories and parts in which things differ so during the group meeting you can reiterate what was told to see where information may be missing. You must stay neutral always and plan the group meetings in a space that has a calm setting, so that it is easier to redirect the conversation to a calmer tone, if necessary. Keep employees focused on the issue at hand instead of going off topic about other issues that do not relate to the one at hand.

Set expectations, so that employees know what behaviors are acceptable and what are not. Stress the importance of respect, and allow every voice and opinion to be heard. Pay close attention to the body language each party gives off. The energy of aggression or dismissal can escalate a situation. Keep notes so that all topics are covered, and everything is cleared up before the day ends. And finally, allow your team to collectively come up with a solution that can help both parties and reiterate the roles they will play in order to execute the solution.

Team Tools

For a team to start to act and work as a unit, they should have different team building activities that promote the different skills you are trying to emphasize. In order to plan these events first you must define the team goals. Have a meeting to create a list of the objectives that can help reach the end goal. Create a collaborative atmosphere that allows all team members to participate in the decision-making process. Hire a professional to facilitate the event. You want to be able to participate in the activities as well and have a neutral voice watch over the event so things can run smoothly where all members are involved are equal partners. Have the event in a neutral space. The event should be held at a facility outside of the office, so it can be more focused on the team members and the activity, and not limited by the space and tone of the office. Finally, ask all employees to provide feedback on their thoughts of the activity, things they struggled with, or just concerns that arise, so that the next team building activity can be improved upon. The overall goal is to have everyone in the team constantly involved in all parts of the team building planning because it puts them in a smaller team building activity of brainstorming and implementation before the big event occurs.

Team Types

Wu-Tang Clan's expansion took off after they started adding other artists and markets under their brand. They grew to have 12 groups and 40 solo artists apart of the Wu-Tang Clan brand. In organizations, you may find that the teams are portrayed in different versions: the virtual and the traditional. There are both virtual and traditional versions of cross-functional and cross-cultural teams.

Performance is considered a major key to the success of teams and organizations. Virtual and traditional teams all rely on performance in order to measure success. In order to fully enhance the effectiveness of these teams, you should first develop a team charter. Virtual teams do not share a common native language, time zone, or country and usually have different managers. This means that many problems can occur due to lack of communication or trust amongst these kinds of groups, so creating a team charter is crucial. Develop team coherence and unity. Communicate and demonstrate the desired behavior and expectation for the team members so no confusion can occur. Also, provide support, information, and needed resources. Performance can be improved in both traditional and virtual project teams when team members have access to a variety of training, knowledge bases, electronic resources, and information. Finally, provide and ask for feedback. Providing feedback or asking for feedback in any group could be very useful especially when dealing with members of different cultures. By implementing behavioral and organizational standards, individual efforts to cope with cultural diversity and virtual work environments can be reduced and redirected to the team task as such. With these standards in place, it can be easier to assess the performance of staff members and provide feedback, but also you can receive feedback on what can be more effective in the workplace.

All in all, each team successfully works towards the overall vision of the organization, whether it is the original vision or expansion. The Wu-Tang Clan was hit with many adversities, especially with the death of one of the original members, ODB, in November of 2004. Being a New York native, his death affected many followers and lovers of the Wu-Tang Clan. The living members are still actively seen in the hip-hop community and worldwide. They have many collaborations with music icons and artists like Nas, Mobb Deep, Busta Rhymes, Kanye West, Redman, and more. With 2018 coming to an end, it was announced that the Wu-Tang Clan will be the subject of a 10-part series set to debut on Hulu called *Wu-Tang Saga*. The series will be a scripted drama set in New York City during the early 90s. Alex Tse (the writer of *Superfly* and *Watchmen*) will write and direct the series, and Method Man will be the executive producer. I C O N I C. Method Man said it best:

"I'm taking one for the team
Like Martin Luther King,
Taking one for the dream."
-*"Dirty Mef"* by Method Man

Hip-Hop Teams: Method Man & Redman Edition

The Wu-Tang Clan formed many smaller groups and sparked an emergence of connections that left a mark on hip-hop. In my world, the dynamic duo that emerged and I learned to appreciate as I grew older, was none other than Method Man and Redman. With their hit movie *How High*, they took humor and hip-hop to film in 2002. Both men followed the main vision of the Wu-Tang Clan by expanding their brands as individuals and taking over multiple markets.

Method Man, a rapper, record producer, and actor, is known for his laid-back demeanor and being articulate when needed. He was the first member to release a solo from the Wu-Tang Clan. He is a man of hip-hop, who never compares his success and losses in the hip-hop game because he knew he was producing his best work. (Unconventional, yet very trusting and centered on self.) Ask Method Man how he sees himself in the pecking order of rap bandits and the answer is pure Meth:

"Hmm, I got a pretty big pecker so I guess I'm number one." No argument here. He expanded his career in ways far past his original persona as the raw, outspoken stoner/rapper to that of a businessman who is into the art of entertaining outside of his normal comfort zone. Television critic for the *Los Angeles Times*, Lorraine Ali, captured the work ethic of Method Man in an article focusing on his expansion in the entertainment industry, "If there's anything predictable about the 46-year-old — who showed up to a recent photo shoot in Los Angeles wearing a crisp white, button-down shirt and black designer blazer while carrying a change of clothes in a crumpled-up Trader Joe's bag, it's that he's willing to try anything."

Method Man has acquired much success due to his teamwork with the Wu-Tang Clan and his duo with Redman, and has gained many accolades like platinum records and albums, movies, and Grammy's for his work and collaborations with others.

Redman, a rapper, DJ, record producer, and actor, is the opposite of Method Man as he is the more outspoken, hyper, wittier character of the two. Redman's rapping made him a hip-hop legend, for sure, but he also has an entertaining personality that keeps your attention. He was not a member of the Wu-Tang Clan but an extension due to being close friends with Method Man. (He was affiliated with Def Squad, which included artists like Erick Sermon aka E Double and Keith Murray, as well as the hip-hop collective Hit Squad which included both members from Def Squad, EPMD, K-Solo, and a few others). Redman expanded his brand through markets of television, hosting VH1's *Scared Famous*, acting, and fashion. He is best known for his accolades individually, his feature productions that crossed over with hit albums from other huge hip-hop artists and groups (Snoop Dogg, Wu-Tang Clan, LL Cool J, and more), as well as his television and film features like his major role in *Seed of Chucky*.

Together this duo has gone on to produce music with my top two favorite artists Biggie and Tupac. They appeared on Tupac's multi-platinum album *All Eyes On Me*, recording "Got My Mind Made Up," and Biggie's posthumous double-platinum album *Born Again*. They have starred in their own television sitcom *Method & Red*, as well as made appearances in video games like *Def Jam Vendetta*, *Def Jam Fight for NY*, and *Def Jam Icon*, often as tag team partners, and on a popular Nickelodeon cartoon show, *The Fairly OddParents*. They have also gone on to produce two albums together under Def Jam Records, *Blackout!* and *Blackout! 2*, with each bringing their own personalities and swag to their iconic brand. It's no surprise they gained a large following. Method Man and Redman have proven to be a successful example of a hip-hop team with their high-performance teamwork.

Now wait... hold up... (listens for door)

My team just pulled up...

TRAPPPP YERRRRRRRRRR!!!!!
(calls out)
YERRRRRRRRRRR
(replies echo)
It's about that time ladies (sparks jotty takes a pull... exhales)
'Roll that shit, Smoke that shit, Pass that Shit!'

- quote from How High

CHAPTER 5

IMPROVING CUSTOMER RELATIONS

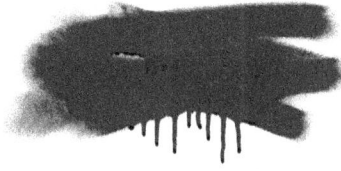

"Nah, nah I never doubted myself. I go into it knowing I'm one of the baddest motherfuckers to ever live. You know, not even in a cocky way, I just feel like I'm one of the baddest motherfuckers to ever walk the face of the earth, you know–and that's just how I am. Cause I feel I AM. I am one of the baddest motherfuckers to ever walk the face of the earth. That's just a fact.
That's just a pure fact."

–Sean "P. Diddy" Combs

Sean "P. Diddy" Combs, a rapper, singer, songwriter, actor, record producer, and entrepreneur, is a major part of hip-hop as we know it. He has gone on to develop himself in different markets of business from music, fashion, hospitality, movies, theater, and education. He is recorded to have accumulated over $820 milliondollars in his businesses and has not done anything to show he intends to stop anytime soon.

P. Diddy is best known for his market takeovers: Music mogul (Bad Boy Records), Fashion mogul (Sean Jean), and Liquor mogul (Ciroc).

I was introduced to P. Diddy as 'Puff Daddy', the right-hand man to the Notorious B.I.G. However, it's kind of funny when I heard from my father how he remembered P. Diddy as a young party promoter back in the day. He is no stranger to reaching the masses and building a brand that shows his concern and care for his community. In *Forbes* magazine, P. Diddy described his take on customer service and how it has helped him thrive in business, "I started my business career at age 12, delivering newspapers. I had a lot of elderly customers, so I would always put the newspaper in between the screen door and the door – that caring made me different, made me better than the last paperboy. Since then, I've always understood that if I give the customers my best and service them differently, whether music, clothing or vodka, I'll get a return on my hard work."

This mentality changed the game for P. Diddy, especially with his ten rules to success and belief in himself. Many of his rules have the same theme of being authentic and creating what you love, something that I found as a leader is the greatest trait to have. His positive outlook and way of thinking have proven to benefit him in all aspects of life. Let's get to the Benjamins...

**SEAN COMBS'S
10 RULES FOR SUCCESS**

1. #BELIEVE
2. RAMP IT UP
3. LOVE WHAT YOU ARE DOING
4. LOCK IN ON YOUR DREAMS
5. BE AROUND INFORMATION
6. YOU CAN NOT ACHIEVE SUCCESS WITHOUT FAILURE
7. IF THERE ISN'T A LITTLE BIT OF FEAR, THEN YOU CAN'T BE FEARLESS
8. ALWAYS KNOW THE REALITY
9. DO WHAT IS ORGANIC TO YOU
10. NEVER LOSE SIGHT OF YOUR DREAMS

"Now, what y'all wanna do?
Wanna be ballers, shot callers, brawlers"
–"All About the Benjamins" Remix by
Puff Daddy and the Family

Customer Service Characteristics

In order to acquire the Benjamins (money) or as we now call it 'get the coin', organizations must have great customer relations. When companies put their focus on creating customer value, they undoubtedly will experience a better financial bottom line. When customers are given great service, client referrals increase, and customers return. The first step in providing great customer service comes down to the choice of customer service candidates for the job.

When looking to employ customer service representatives, it is important to look for these personal characteristics and competencies:

Attentiveness: Being attentive to customers as well as the details in their requests are crucial. According to writer and marketing strategist, Gregory Cotti, in his article on the "16 Customer Service Skills That Every Employee Needs," it's important to pay attention to individual customer interactions (watching the language/terms that they use to describe their problems), but it's also important to be mindful and attentive to the feedback that you receive at large. Being attentive allows things to get handled in a faster and more efficient manner.

Communication Skills: Communication should be clear and concise. Customers should be able to understand the message being delivered. Cotti also stated that it is important to be cautious about how some of your communication habits translate to customers, and it's best to err on the side of caution whenever you find yourself questioning a situation.

Knowledge of the Product: Always know the product at hand. If there is a question that cannot be answered, provide help by directing customers to an employee with knowledge on that topic.

Time Management Skills: Spend enough time with the customer so that their issues can be resolved. If you cannot help that customer, know when to ask for assistance and point the customer in the direction of an employee who can assist them.

Handling Surprises: When in customer service, you are interacting with many different people from different races and backgrounds.Think on your feet and provide aide wherever you can.

Customer-Driven Mindset

A customer-driven mindset focuses on the values that customers hold. To push this type of mindset throughout an organization, the customer service leader is imperative. As a leader of an organization, you should coach your team to implement and carry out the same vision. Managers select, train, coach, and support employees to develop the performance competencies needed to achieve a customer-driven company mission. In order to do this, you should raise awareness and set expectations and standards of behavior for your employees. Train and coach managers on the expectations and behaviors for proper customer service. Present the guidelines for the ethics of customer relations for all employees.

Managers advise employees to develop efficient, cost-effective, and customer-driven processes. In order to do this, you should identify and eliminate barriers and obstacles that may arise. Guide employees on finding issues in their systems that can be solved or improved. Listen to the feedback from cus-

tomers about the organization's service. Use this information to improve other areas of customer service that can improve financial value.

Managers model, promote, and develop company-wide, customer-driven teamwork. In order to do this, you should learn and develop skills, and reinforce and support continuous improvement amongst your team. Model and continue to promote expected behaviors. Develop company-wide, customer-driven team building exercises and goals for your organization's subgroups and for the organization. Continue to provide the necessary support for the completion of goals.

Customer Communication

We have spoken about communication within the workplace and amongst leadership, so let's cover the proper way to communicate with customers. In hip-hop, the message is conveyed in different ways (music, art, performances, apparel, etc.). Each thread of communication is carefully developed in order to have a massive impact on society. Some communications are bringing awareness to the current state of the organization, while others offer examples of hope or change. However, each communication should follow the same guidelines in order to be effective:

- Know your audience
- Share your objective
- Be an active listener
- Be aware of nonverbal communication
- Build trust

In hip-hop, communication is imperative because it showcases the thoughts and feelings of the artist. If the message is not properly communicated it can be shown to promote the wrong image. For example, a lot of music today may be considered to promote drug use and the glorification of gun violence. Listening to this music may have a negative reaction from people of an older generation, whereas the younger generation may praise and acknowledge these messages more often.

At times, customer service representatives may have to deal with customers over the telephone, through email, web chats, or in-store. In any organization, having proper telephone etiquette is crucial because you are providing a service to customers. As more companies adopt a customer-centric focus, customer service expectations have increased. As a result, customer support quality has quickly become a distinguishing factor between a company's success and failure. When dealing with customers who you may not have face-to-face contact with, these few tips will greatly benefit your organization:

Listen: Listening is an important factor in customer communication. It is important to listen to the tones and words that are used by yourself and the customer.

Challenge the negative thoughts: Break down the words and phrases used during self-talk and modify them to view things from a more positive perspective. In this sense, challenge the thoughts of the customer by asking questions that might highlight positives they may have experienced.

Look at every difficult situation as a problem to be solved: Take a problem-solving stance. In phone etiquette, providing honest answers is very beneficial, unfortunately, not all questions can be answered. If an employee doesn't know the answer, finding the answer from another associate or transferring the customer to a more suitable team member to assist them may be necessary. At that moment the employees are putting the issues of the customer first and trying to provide a solution as quickly as possible.

Use every situation as an opportunity to learn: Providing excellent customer service takes time and proper training. Each customer is a different experience, so in order to be more prepared for future customer service calls, use each call as a learning device to implement in future calls.

Build Customer Relationships

Every customer service experience should be based on building a relationship with your customers. Each customer is unique and provides a different value to an organization. To build these relationships it takes time, patience, but beneficial in the end. By adopting the following actions and strategies, you can build customer service relationships:

Know more about your customers: When you know your customers, you can better assist them and they can recognize your dedication to helping them.

Be honest always: Being honest helps to build trust between the employee and customer as well and build their relationship.

Connect with customers regularly: Having a connection with customers show you are constantly interested in their experiences and it helps build on their relationship.

"Don't think of yourself as my husband. Think of yourself as my marriage customer service agent."

Build Trust with your customers: Without trust you cannot build a healthy successful relationship or partnership.

Focus on customer complaints: Customer complaints can be used as a tool to monitor and adjust behaviors when dealing with clients. It can improve customer relations when complaints are acknowledged and cascaded throughout the organization.

Problem-Solve with Unhappy Customers

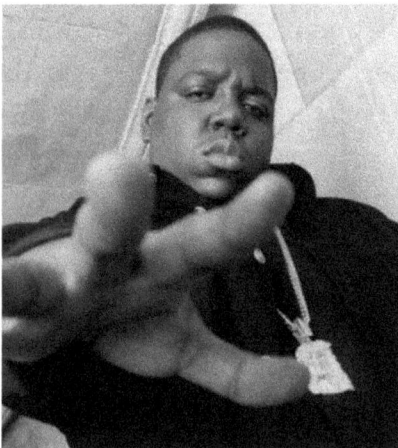

"Spread love,

it's the Brooklyn way"

-Notorious B.I.G.

The Notorious B.I.G. aka Biggie Smalls, fellow Brooklyn native and hip-hop legend, was known for his raw lyrics about the drug game and his struggle to get on top. He and Tupac were heavily played in my household growing up. There was no rivalry between the East Coast and West Coast that could prevent each artist from gracing the speaker system in my basement. I can still hear my parents telling my brothers, "If I hear your sister repeat any curse word, I'm tearing y'all up!"

Biggie's raw delivery didn't stop him from being loved and his death was a heavy hit to the hip-hop community. Many people flooded the streets on the day of his funeral, blasting his music over the speakers and chanting his name. That's the Brooklyn way. Ironically enough, I chose the line above from his hit song, "Juicy" because he captured the nature of having the odds against him and then turning it around to reach for success. He encountered both negative and positive experiences during his short career and will ultimately be remembered for the positive contributions he brought to hip-hop.

Now let's flip to the business side of things. There will be a balance of good and bad customer service experiences within an organization. Problem-solving is one of the biggest tools you can use to gain trust and build a relationship. Learning how to problem-solve with both happy and unhappy customers is valuable to your business. The best way to do this would be actively doing these small steps:

- Actively listening
- Acknowledge the customer concerns
- Build rapport
- Solve a problem in a timely fashion
- Remain calm
- Follow up

The most important step in customer service is actively listening. Listen with understanding and sympathy. The next step is to acknowledge the customers' concerns. When customers know that you understand their issues and are willing to help them the best way possible, it can change their tense emotional state to a more relaxed one. To understand the emotional state of yourself and others it is imperative first to understand emotional intelligence. There are three main steps to boosting your emotional intelligence:

Calibration: learn to track signs of yourself and other emotional states

Regulation: learning to regulate the emotional brain

Communication: mastering language patterns

"Yes, I think I have good people skills.
What kind of idiot question is that?"

Building a rapport with your customer builds trust and ensures their satisfaction at the end of their experience with you. Try to solve their problem in a timely fashion. Customers do not like to wait for extended times. If the problem cannot be solved, know when to ask for help with a more suitable fellow employee.

During confusing and tense situations, it is important for the customer service representative to remain calm. Not only is a calm demeanor important for the customer service representative, but it is also important for the customer to be calm as well. A distressed customer can make handling an issue a little harder, and can come in different forms such as antagonizing and instigating. With these types of customers sometimes it is best to part ways with them or resort back to your community guidelines and create an email communicating the issue and why the customer's actions violate your community guidelines. For customers who always have a complaint, it's best to find out the root cause of their complaints. The best ways to deal with a distressed customer are to:

- Calm them down
- Communicate understandingly of the problem and empathize
- Give a hearty "thank you!" when it's over

Finally, after everything is resolved, a good customer representative should follow up with their customer. Finding out if the customer is satisfied with the resolution, you can learn if the customer has any complaints or has positive feedback about their experience.

Customer Feedback

Customer service feedback is a great device for monitoring and making improvements within the organization. Gathering customer feedback can take form in many different assessment tools: focus groups, survey questionnaires, online reviews, etc. Customer service questionnaires are brief surveys used to focus on both service and product satisfaction. These surveys are usually no more than 10 questions with a scale used to rank scores, and may include some "open-ended" questions on thoughts to improve customer service. Here are five ways to collect customer feedback data using customer survey questionnaires:

Customer Service Advantage: Get Customer Feedback

How do we know our customers are happy with us?

Just ask them. That's how we know we're doing a good job and more importantly, what we can do to even be better.

Copyright © MAXIII Shop Hoken

- Ask for a few moments of their time to fill out the questionnaire
- Include the questionnaire with the receipt, by asking the customer to mail it back or bring it back to store during the next visit
- Use a survey questionnaire to interview customers while they are leaving
- Mail surveys to a random sample of customers
- Hold customer focus groups

Focus groups are a little more complex in that they require planning to implement the program and evaluation of customer satisfaction. They are an effective way of gathering data about customer opinions and provide direct feedback. There are three parts to running a focus group: planning, recruiting participants, and running the focus group. When running the focus group, details go into making sure the customer has given consent to participate and it is also important to provide a neutral space, and a moderator to ensure no one person is dominating the group. In order to run a successful focus group, the following steps can help:

- Hand out consent forms and any other paperwork needed before the focus group begins
- Allow participants to introduce themselves
- Share the purpose of the meeting
- Ask questions to help guide discussions
- Stay neutral and empathetic
- Write down their responses or record sessions
- Prevent individuals from dominating the conversation

- Diffuse escalated situations
- Limit meeting to an hour and a half the most.
- Allow participants to share feedback and review it
- Debrief with the assistant
- Repeat focus groups with new participants

With these different assessment tools, the amount of information you can gather is endless. However, you should not only limit these assessments for customer feedback for just external customers, but you should also implement them amongst your internal customers as well. Every person in your organization is a great tool for feedback. When you pay attention to the feedback from your customers, both internal and external, you can provide a better service. Actively listen to their opinions or complaints and show understanding and interest in solving the issue, and your customers will build trust and a rapport with you. In the end, the result will be loyal repeating customers and a source of referrals to new customers, which will grow our business.

Develop Customer Loyalty

Overall, all these tools can help you develop a long-term customer loyalty. Customer loyalty is one of the biggest keys in having a successful organization. Loyal customers are returning customers or advocates for your company or product and can drive more business in your direction. In hip-hop, especially within Sean "P. Diddy" Combs and Bad Boy Records, customer loyalty grew steadily, with new customers joining daily. Loyal customers of hip-hop, keep the culture growing and thriving through more than transactional sales, but now through downloads, social media shares, and retweets. Different platforms allow hip-hop to be displayed and broadcasted to the masses through organizations of their own. Some of these platforms may include Snapchat,

Twitter, Instagram, and Facebook to name a few. These platforms now gain a loyal customer base from hip-hop because they are delivering information about the culture in real time.

Micah Solomon (customer service consultant, keynote speaker, and author of High-Tech, High-Touch Customer Service) states that building customer loyalty starts by putting the customer at the center of everything concerning the organization, "at the center of your company or department, your daily routines, the way you hire, the way you design your webforms." Solomon identifies four elements that make up the framework for building satisfied customers:

- A "perfect product or service"
- Caring delivery
- Timely delivery
- An effective problem resolution process

In addition to building customer satisfaction brand ambassadors (or influencers) are important. Providing a platform for your customers to be engaged and advocate for your product is useful. Solomon calls this homebuilding, when creating an environment, product, process or service that "feels like home" to your customer. Developing long-term customer loyalty is seen by your internal employees, and fosters confidence in your product within the organization and by empowering your internal customers will allow your employees to perform at their best. Following are various ways you can empower your employees:

Talk to your employees and ask them to brainstorm on ways to improve service. Provide incentives for ideas that are chosen. This would encourage people to have a problem-solving mindset.

Rotate employees so they can learn different parts of the organization. Employees who end up knowing more about every department of the organization, are less bored and more motivated.

Develop unity among the leadership team and provide outside activities that can take members away from the workplace. This places everyone on the same level and encourages teamwork.

Get to know your employees on an individual basis. This will allow employees to feel more comfortable and build trust.

Now let me ask a serious question…

Do you know what loyalty looks like?

"Remember Rappin' Duke, duh-ha duh-ha
You never thought that hip-hop would take it this far"

- "Juicy" by Notorious B.I.G.

In hip-hop, loyalty is the bloodline of the community. Unfortunately, loyalty is often displayed when tragedy strikes. I was only three turning four when Biggie died in 1997. However, I still relive those moments growing up hearing tributes to Biggie on the radio, seeing murals drawn, and watching documentaries about his life. P. Diddy, Bad Boy Records, and their loyal fan base did nothing short to keep his legacy alive.

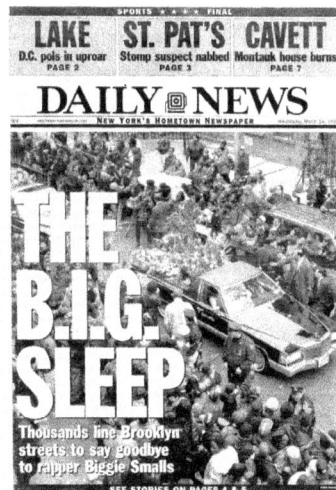

During his funeral procession, thousands of fans celebrated his life by taking to the streets of Brooklyn. We recently passed the twenty-year milestone since he passed, and his music is still trending. It's always a question, what hip-hop would be like today if great legends like Biggie, Tupac, Aaliyah, Lisa "Left Eye" Lopez, Nate Dogg, Big Pun, Big L, ODB, etc. were still here today. If you got asked today, "Where does your loyalty lie?"

For me it's quite simple, always involving hip-hop and my true Native American roots.

ONLY CHRISTOPHER WE ACKNOWLEDGE IS WALLACE

YEEEEEEEEEEEEEERRRRRRRRRRRRRRRRRRRRR

Bad Boy Entertainment Customer Relations

The year 1993 was the year of the 'Greats' ... Bad Boy Records was founded by Sean "P. Diddy" Combs. This evolutionary label had some of the most impactful and greatest artists of that period. Their entertainment roster was stacked with heavy hitters like Notorious B.I.G., Faith Evans, 112, New Edition, The Lox, Danity Kane, Day 26, Total, Young Joc, Shyne, Mase, Carl Thomas, Foxy Brown, Cassie, Machine Gun Kelly, French Montana, and so on. They had many affiliates that extended the family with Lil' Kim, Usher, Justin Beiber, Bow Wow, Mario Winans, Stevie J, LL Cool J, Ryan Leslie, and the list continues. The Bad Boy brand that P. Diddy created embodied what he believed was a customer-driven organization. The artists and label built great customer relationships that still carry over to the present day.

Bad Boy Records had many successful joint ventures with other labels like Arista Records, and most recently Universal Records, accumulating over hundreds of millions of dollars. "Bad Boy's annual sales have reached an overall average of $100 million with more than $75 million records sold worldwide by an impressive artist roster." (Bad Boy Entertainment). Many of the records and albums that were produced by Bad Boy Records went on to become Platinum or Gold Certified and have the potential to go on to become Diamond Certified. Biggie's posthumous *Life After Death* was the first and only Bad Boy Records to be currently certified Diamond. Aside from music, Diddy expanded the Bad Boy brand with his collaboration with MTV for the *Making the Band* series. This opened the doors for many of their consumers and fans to really get to know artists on a personal level. With the tours, performances, the meet and greets, and so on, the connection with both external and internal consumers were off the charts. In the *Los Angeles Times*, artist "Machine Gun" Kelly (internal customer) stated, "Bad Boy showed us it could be deeper than music. It showed us we could make our own clothes, make our own cologne. We can make bigger moves than music." Bad Boy Entertainment was involved in different music-related subsidiaries like managing other music producers, music writers, recording studios, and so on. Each subsidiary is widely known and sought after, as well as generating millions of dollars annually. The Janice Combs Management subsidiary (Janice Combs is the mother of P. Diddy) manages music producers in the industry and generates income of more than $10 million a year. One of New York's most innovative, state of the art, full-service recording studios, Daddy's House Studios, has been used for many Bad Boy's recordings and other outside projects.

As far as the external customers, fans are able to relive the glory days of the top artists in the 90s and 2000s at different performances and collaborations over the years. Each event reinforces their brand identity, builds trust, exposes them to a larger loyal fan base worldwide. Their reception at the 2015 BET Awards Show was a pivotal moment for their 20th anniversary as a label. The *Los Angeles Times* described the crowd reception of reunion at the BET Awards Show by saying, "Artists who ruled the airwaves throughout the 90s and early 2000s — Faith Evans, Mase, Lil' Kim, the Lox and 112 — charmed the audience of R&B icons and new rap upstarts out of their seats. The crowd sang along in unison, the music part of their DNA." From the awards show, P. Diddy orchestrated the Bad Boy Tour in 2016 that traveled throughout the country touching 25 cities. In 2017, they joined the Tribeca Film Festival, bringing their roots back to their hometown of New York and paying homage to where the label emerged in Harlem and Brooklyn. The show was completely sold out, premiering the *Can't Stop, Won't Stop: The Bad Boy Story* documentary alongside an iconic performance with a lineup that included Total, Carl Thomas, Mario Winans, Faith Evans, Mase, Lil' Kim, the Lox, 112, and P. Diddy himself.

For P. Diddy and Bad Boy Entertainment **'It Was All A Dream'** . Starting from nothing and rising to the top, they faced adversity, **'Mo Money, Mo Problems'**. Even with one of the biggest losses in hip-hop history with the death of Biggie, they continued to push through: **'Can't Nobody Hold Me Down'**. And their legacy lives on with the **'Can't Stop, Won't Stop'** mantra that embodies Diddy and Bad Boy Entertainment. Loyal fans like myself, will never allow the legacy to die out, 'cause once you join Bad Boy, you're a **'Bad Boy for Life'**.

CHAPTER 6

RESEARCH METHODOLOGY

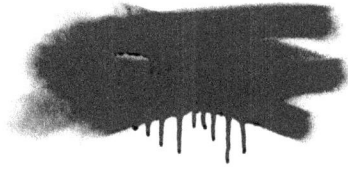

Ooooo the good ol' teenage years...

The time for first loves, high school sweethearts, breakups, puberty, self-exploration, and development of confidence. No worries of bills or crazy work deadlines. This is the creation period of the ego. The time where people normally set the tone for how they will be perceived in life as either a "popular kid" or a "nerd." With a host of influences in media, music, and peers to introducing the young and naïve teens to the life of money, drugs, alcohol, and sex. Hip-hop spiked many areas targeting every struggle I experienced on a daily basis. During this period, some of my favorite artists like Lil Wayne, Kanye West, Jay-Z, and T.I. released music that hit home for me in more ways than one. Hip-hop artists collaborated with many R&B and Pop artists to create what I called "hip-hop love songs" which became an all-time favorite of mine, and breakup songs at that time seemed to speak my feelings better than I ever could.

UNCONVENTIONAL & ICONIC

Research Methods in Industrial Organizational Psychology

I was introduced to different mental states of being through seeing various changes in my friends that didn't fully understand at this point, but my natural ability to listen and help my peers was undeniable. This only gravitated me more towards to studying psychology in college. In Industrial Organizational Psychology, research is used to help organizations flourish. Research methods are important in studying human behavior to give insights, describe, predict, and explain different occurrences in the workplace. According to John Creswell, an American academic known for his work in mixed methods research, stated that there are four philosophical worldviews:

Four Worldviews for Research

Postpositivism	Constructivism
▪Determination ▪Reductionism ▪Empirical observation and measurement ▪Theory verification	▪Understanding ▪Multiple participant meanings ▪Social and historical construction ▪Theory generation
Advocacy/Participatory	**Pragmatism**
▪Political ▪Empowerment issue-oriented ▪Collaborative ▪Change-oriented	▪Consequences of actions ▪Problem-centered ▪Pluralistic ▪Real-world practice oriented

Postpositivism: Reflects a deterministic philosophy in which the causes of something probably determine the effects or outcomes; this position is better known as the "scientific method" or quantitative research.

Constructivism: Reflects the nature of knowledge. It is based on assumptions and ideas of individuals, and the meaning they developed through their experiences from day-to-day as well as their interactions with others.

Advocacy/Participatory: Reflects that research investigation needs to connect with politics or a political agenda. The research will contain an agenda focused on specific issues that may alter the lives of the participants, the institutions or communities they live or work, as well as the life and perspective of the researcher.

Pragmatism: Reflects the actions, situations, and consequences. The main focus is the problem; finding ways to understand, develop, and gain an understanding of the problem.

After much experience in the educational management and leadership sector, I grew to find a passion for revamping businesses, the programs and systems within them, and coaching and mentoring staff to be more effective. I have found that many issues come from the structure and leadership of a program or business, and then trickle down to affect the consumers as well as employees. In this case, the philosophical worldview of pragmatism is most fitting for me. I am focused on figuring out the problems amongst organizations, individuals, and teams, trying to learn more about the problem to create a solution. I used mixed research methods in order to find solutions for my organization. The different tests I conducted to find the problems within the organization were both qualitative and quantitative as well as subjective and objective. The approach I would take opened the doors for a lot of data to be collected and educated decisions being made.

The Research Process

So let's break down these High School years...

In 2006, I entered high school, young, naïve, and very much comfortable with being focused on academics and sports. Walking down the hallways of a Catholic high school but bringing my styles of hip-hop with the latest Jordan's to go with my uniform, my North Face bookbag and coat during the winter months, my nameplate chain and ring. Quiet, yet popular, and part of the leaders of the step team. Acquainted with every crew in school, but my crew was different. We came from different backgrounds, all unique in our own way, just girls who banned together as the outcasts in the school only to become a leading group amongst our peers. I built myself on focus, determination, and drive. I had a steady routine: go to school, go to practice, go to work, and then home. My 128 GB iPod always charged, and headphones were always blasting music. Jay-Z released his album *Kingdom Come*, November 2006 and was the precursor of albums I would constantly listen to throughout high school.

During sophomore year, the two hit albums that were frequently played on bus rides home and during practice were Jay-Z's *American Gangster* album and Kanye West's *Graduation*album. Jay-Z's album was based on the epic movie *American Gangster* starring Denzel Washington (hip-hop and theater collabo-

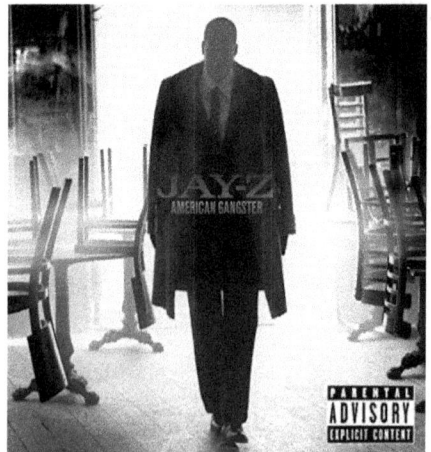

ration). This album was a crazy start of many collaborations in the years to follow with Jay-Z, Diddy, Lil Wayne, T.I., and Kanye West.

Now in terms of Industrial Organizational Psychology, the research process is summarized in a five-step cycle.

The Empirical Research Cycle

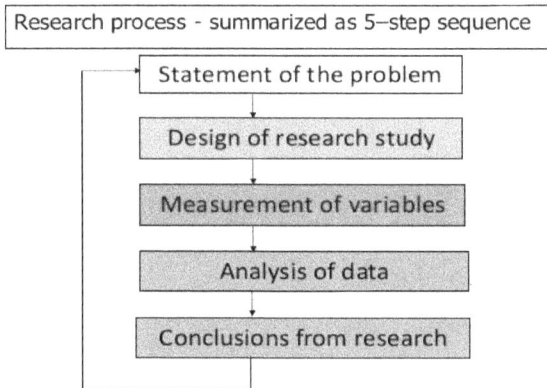

Research process - summarized as 5–step sequence
Statement of the problem
Design of research study
Measurement of variables
Analysis of data
Conclusions from research

Statement of Purpose

The best start is to state the problem you are focusing on in a Statement of Purpose. As a researcher you would create a theory (theoretical lens) using either the inductive or deductive method. A theoretical lens transforms the perspective of the study and shapes the types of questions asked, informs how data is collected and analyzed, and provides a call for action or change. Now let me quickly break down the two. The inductive method is a research process in which conclusions are drawn about a class of objects or people based on a knowledge of a specific member of the class being investigated (from specific to general), it is a method of discovery. The deductive method is a research process in which conclusions are drawn about a specific member of a class of objects of people based on knowledge of the general class under investigation (general to specific), it is a method of verification and explanation. By stating the purpose of the study, a research question and hypothesis can be created in order to guide the research process.

Design of Research

In 2008, T.I. hit the scene with his *Paper Trail* album that housed the single "Swagger Like Us" featuring Lil Wayne, Kanye West, and Jay-Z. This song was the anthem for all crews in high school. Talk about theme music! With our first black president, Barack Obama, hip-hop skyrocketed with this new influence. The presidential election was by far the biggest one ever. Young Jeezy released "My President" featuring Nas, which became the anthem for Obama's first term in office.

ICONIC

Lil Wayne and Jay-Z teamed up for *The Carter III* project, which was the theme for many of my ringtones on the epic T-Mobile Sidekick. The Sidekick was the first premature form of what we see now as Twitter and Facebook, where the away messages always told your mood. It was like holding a handheld computer keyboard that comes in different editions and has special lighting features, mainly used as the second phone for kids in my era. It was the best way to start drama in different schools and broadcast a relationship, your away message had to always be on point.

When designing research there are four types of research methods that can be used: laboratory (experimental), quasi-experimental, questionnaire (survey), and observation.

Survey studies provide a quantitative (numeric) description of trends, attitudes, or opinions of a population by studying a sample of that population. With these results are retrieved from the sample questioned, researchers draw conclusions about the population as a whole. Experimental quantitative studies can use samples like a survey study, however they differ because researchers use experimental studies to research the cause and effect of a particular item, and how to control outside factors that can cause change as well. According to John Creswell, the basic intent of an experimental design is to test the impact of a treatment (or an intervention) on an outcome, controlling for all other factors that might influence that outcome." Both study types can be conducted by collecting data from one particular time or data collected over time. In the case of surveys, they call this cross-sectional (data collected at one point in time) or longitudinal (data collected over time). In a quasi-experimental research study, there would not be a random selection for participants. Designation to conditions (treatment versus no treatment or comparison) is by means of self-selection (by which participants choose treatment for themselves) or administrator selection (e.g., by officials, teachers, policymakers and so on) or both of these routes.

When implementing a study, you must identify the type of sample to use. Is the choice of sample randomly chosen or specifically chosen? These factors determine if the individuals of each study play a huge role in the outcome since they are all unique. Decide if you will be collecting this information at one point in time or over a duration of time. Depending on the situation, the organization needs to know if you are just generalizing the sample to a specific population or are testing for more data. Figure out if testing for a specific outcome based on cause and effect, and if there are factors that can cause a similar change. There can be a simple cause and effect exchange, however there can also be small minor factors that can create that same outcome.

Observation qualitative studies are when the researcher takes notes on the behavior and activities of individuals they are researching at the site. Like interview qualitative studies, they make use of general unstructured open-ended questions that allow participants to provide their opinions openly. Interview qualitative studies differ from observation qualitative studies in that the researcher conducts face-to-face interviews with participants, telephone interviews, or engages in small focus group interviews that normally contain six to eight interviewees in each group.

When deciding which design to implement in a study, an organization needs to take into consideration how much control they want over the information they are retrieving as well as knowing the type of information they are trying to retrieve. Do they want the setting to be more natural or in a facility? Is the information they are trying to retrieve difficult for people to discuss or does the information have to be observed?

As a consultant, I place most of my confidence in the observation research method. This method, like all methods, have both advantages and limitations. John Creswell affirmed that researchers are able to get a firsthand experience with the participants, they can record information as it occurs, and they are able to notice unusual aspects during observations. This research tool is useful in covering topics that are uncomfortable for participants to discuss.

Measurement of Variables

By senior year, I knew what I wanted to do. Jay-Z dropped *The Blueprint 3* at the beginning of the school year in 2009. It's funny how that album greatly reflected how I was growing as a person. The lyricism in the album showed great maturity and growth in Jay-Z as an artist. In a 2009 interview about *The Blueprint 3* Jay-Z stated: "With *The Blueprint 3*, I wanted to make what I call a new classic. I wanted to make an album that was fresh and dealt with current events. I wanted to go back to the thought pattern of making music with lush arrangements. I'm just doing my thing to add to the diversity of our genre."

I, on the other hand, was focused on preparing myself for college majoring in psychology. "So Ambitious" featuring Pharrell was on repeat as my song for motivation. By 2010, I graduated high school with honors, a full semester of college credits, about to start college in the fall, and my high school sweetheart and I were attached at the hip. And then BOOM!!!

PUBERTY & HEARTBREAK!

Puberty hit me at the age of 17 (late bloomer, I'm honestly convinced it was more like 21... but that's debatable according to my mother) and I didn't experience much heartbreak in high school. But that feeling would knock the wind out of almost anybody. Emotions hit, distance from home, new environment, heartbreak, and a ton of other factors (variables) started taking a toll on me. Perfect timing for Kanye West to drop his My Dark Twisted Fantasy album in November. This album matched the struggles of heartbreak. I went from an Honors student to a 2.4 GPA (mental and emotional breakdown... commencing.... NOW). I was going through a breakup and puberty (emotional wreck is an understatement), my beautiful long thick hair was falling out from the stress and new change in environment (by far the worst blow to a woman's self-confidence), and isolation.

Enters Mortal Combat Arena

Depression kicks in, in 5... 4... 3... 2 ... 1

Let's sprinkle some anxiety

FINISH HIM !!

Top it all off with a blow of new underlying health issues

FRESHMAN STARTER PACK 101

In research, the variables that you use are the ones you focus on in your study. Variables can come in different forms: independent/dependent, predictor/criterion, or categorical/quantitative.

1. **Independent/Dependent**

   - Independent variables are those that are manipulated or controlled by the researcher during the research experiment.
   - Dependent variables are usually the variable of interest to the researcher and are often an aspect of behaviors or attitudes.

2. **Predictor/Criterion**

   - Predictor variables are used to predict or forecast a criterion variable.
   - Criterion variables are the primary objects of a research study.

3. Categorical/Quantitative

- Categorical variables (gender, race) are not inherently numerical but can be coded to have a numerical meaning.
- Quantitative variables (age, time) are inherently numerical and therefore the number does carry a value.

Scales are commonly used to assess the data that is recorded. There are four different types of scales:

Nominal scale of measurement is categorical data and numbers that are simply used as identifiers.

An **ordinal scale** of measurement represents an ordered series of relationships or rank order and allows comparisons of the degree to which two subjects possess the dependent variable.

Interval scale of measurement are numerical scales where intervals have the same interpretation throughout.

Ratio scale of measurement is a combination of the previous three scales. It provides a name or category for each object (the numbers serve as labels), the objects are ordered (in terms of the ordering of the numbers), and the same difference at two places on the scale has the same meaning. However, this scale also has an absolute zero (no numbers exist below zero).

Measurement Scales

Scale	Order	Distance	True Zero	Examples
Nominal	no	no	no	Color, Gender, Ethnicity, Country
Ordinal	yes	no	no	Rating scales, Rank orders
Interval	yes	yes	no	Time of day, Year, IQ, Likert scales
Ratio	yes	yes	yes	Age, Height, Weight, Rates

Data Analysis

The data collected may come in a variety of forms such as survey answers, video recorded interviews, behavioral assessments, etc. How you present the information in your study relies on what kind of correlational study you are writing. There are three different approaches:

Qualitative Proposal: According to Creswell, in qualitative research, no one structure for a qualitative proposal prevails. It is outlined with an introduction (statement of the problem, the purpose of the study, research questions), procedures, preliminary pilot findings (if available), expected impact and significance of the study, and references. A Qualitative proposal can have a constructive/interpretive or transformative model, meaning that it is broken down to transform or interpret findings. It stands out with the section of procedures detailing assumptions, roles, narration and strategies used for validating findings. The explanation of the impact and significance of the study constitutes this being a Qualitative proposal.

Quantitative Proposal: is outlined with an introduction (statement of the problem, the purpose of the study, research questions/hypothesis, and theoretical perspectives), review of the literature (theory may be included in this section), methods, preliminary studies or pilot tests, and appendixes. A Quantitative proposal has much of the same design with respect to stating the problem, providing a purpose and revealing the research questions. The difference is the use of the theoretical perspective, the insertion of the literature review and methods used to conduct the study.

Mixed Methods Proposal: Creswell affirmed that in a mixed methods design format, the researcher brings together approaches that are included in both the quantitative and qualitative formats. It is outlined with an introduction (research problem, the purpose of the project/rationale for a mixed methods study, research questions and hypotheses, philosophical foundations), literature review, methods, researcher's resources, and skills to conduct mixed methods research, potential ethical issues, references, and appendixes. The appendix provides additional or supplementary material that is used or created to represent findings in the study.

Conclusions from Research

As a psychology major, of course I tried to diagnose myself. Cause CLEARLY, I'm a 17-year-old psychologist and I knew what I was doing...

HA! JOKE'S ON ME

I later found out that I was looking at all the wrong signs. I FOCUSED ON THE WRONG STUDY! I focused on general aspects of things instead of just focusing on the specific factors similar to my own. Like most people in any change situation or in any organization, understanding the target and goal is necessary in order to get viable results. Having knowledge and background information on certain areas, of any organization, can be very useful when trying to implement change. Now don't get me wrong, studies are very useful. However, like all things, there are limitations. Limitations of a research study based on a methodological approach and research sample can cause the following:

The samplebeing improperly represented: If the sample data is taken wrongly or improperly logged, it can cause errors in the results and data analysis. Improper representation of the target population might hinder or limit the researcher from achieving their desired aims and objectives. Researchers can also address this limitation by making sure they have a valid sample. Making sure the data collection process does not contribute inaccuracies will help ensure the overall quality of subsequent analyses.

Inability to control the environment: Researchers may have a hard time getting unbiased responses from participants. Responses often depend on the time, which is dependent on the conditions occurring during that particular time frame. Participant bias can come from the lack of trust they have for the researchers or their current state, physically, emotionally, or mentally, in the environment they are in. It is very hard for researchers to address this limitation because some approaches are considered unethical, such as not disclosing to participants they are in a study. They could, however, not disclose the purpose of their study, but that can also be seen as unethical.

Research Ethics and Report Writing

Ideally, when conducting a study, gather the best results possible, but also keep in mind the participants you are working with. The American Psychological Association (APA) created a code of ethics that researchers are expected to follow. Based on this code, participants are granted five rights:

1. **Informed consent:** Participants have the right to know the purpose of the research they are participating in as well as the right to decline or withdraw their participation at any time without any negative consequences. Participants should also be notified of any risks associated with their participation in the research.

2. **Privacy:** Participants have the right to their privacy and integrity. Psychologists are guided on how to properly and ethically record data and research with minimal invasion or intrusion of the privacy of each participant.

3. **Confidentiality:** Psychologists are to hold the privacy and confidentiality of their participants as a top priority. Limited information about participants is disclosed to other members or organizations that are interested or aiding in the research. This is also imperative to avoid any bias against participants or vulnerabilities that individuals or group may experience (socioeconomic status, disability, race, religion, etc.).

4. **Protection from deception:** Psychologists are to engage in honest, transparent practices within all aspects of psychology. Participants should have information that can help them in understanding the study, or aid them in making an educated decision to participate in the study.

5. **Debriefing:** Debriefing is used to answer any participant questions related to the research, to remove any harmful effects the study may have created, and to leave participants with a sense of dignity. A proper debriefing provides information about how the study adds to the current knowledge on the topic, how the results might be applied, as the importance of the current study.

Industrial Organization Psychologists would consider the use of deception in conducting an experiment when they do not want the participants to know the purpose of the study. Deception regarding the main purpose of the experiment is often used to avoid the so-called Hawthorne effect. The Hawthorne effect is the tendency of research participants to behave in accordance with what they think the experimenter's expectations are, or to alter their behavior due to their awareness of being observed.

This term was coined by Henry Landsberger (a sociologist) when he analyzed the earlier experiments of a western electric factory, Hawthorne Works, which was conducted by Elton Mayo (a psychologist, industrial researcher, and organizational theorist). According to the Society for Research in Child Development Ethical Standards in Research, when using deception, the researcher needs to consider the following ethical obligations (this goes for both children and adults). Whenever withholding information or deception is judged to be essential to conduct the study, the investigator must ensure that the use of deception is accepted amongst all research team members. If withholding information or deception is practiced, and there is reason to believe that the research participants will be negatively affected by it, adequate measures should be taken after the study to ensure the participant's understanding of the reasons for the deception. Investigators whose research is dependent upon deception should try to employ deception methods that have no known negative effects.

Hip-Hop & Mental Health Awareness

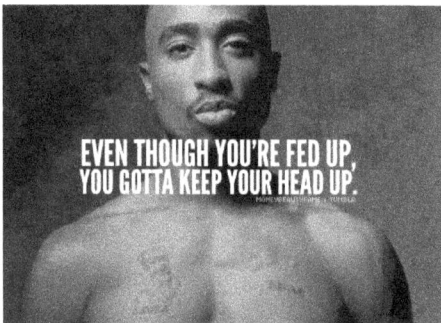

EVEN THOUGH YOU'RE FED UP, YOU GOTTA KEEP YOUR HEAD UP.

Mental health awareness is a heavy topic throughout Industrial Organizational Psychology and other psychology domains. The World Health Organization (WHO) defines mental health as a state of well-being in which every individual realizes his or her own potential, can cope with the normal stresses of life, can work productively and fruitfully, and is able to contribute to her or his community. In many urban areas, mental health is at a low because of lack of resources and knowledge. A report by WHO has calculated that mental disorders account for nearly 12% of the global burden of disease. In her article "Urbanization and Mental Health," that was published in *Industrial Psychiatry Journal*, Kalpana Srivastava states that the burden of mental disorders is maximal in young adults, which are considered to be the most productive age of the population, and there is a meta higher prevalence of mental disorders in urban areas, 80.6%, whereas it was 48.9% in rural areas. These mental disorders primarily composed of depression and neurotic disorders.

Hip-hop personalities are beginning to use their platform to bring awareness about mental disorders and seeking help, through its public figures openly speaking about their personal experiences with mental health issues or through music, art, etc. Since many people in the hip-hop community can relate to the effects of stress and being mentally unhealthy, due to the demands of their jobs, they want to bring awareness to their fans. This new phenomenon is taking place because it is commonly seen that the black community usually does not seek help, much less talk much about mental health issues or have the money/assistance to aid its members.

Hip-HopMethods

Rappers are using social media and lyrics to address their vulnerabilities and even stories with fans. Hip-hop artist Logic, performed at the Video Music Awards his song, "1-800-273-8255," which is named after the National Suicide Prevention Lifeline. Logic who openly discussed having anxiety, has used his music to address the seriousness of mental health and urge people from diverse backgrounds to seek professional assistance.

Kid Cudi, a recording artist and actor, publicly dealt with his mental health disorder, depression, in a more hands-on approach. He took to social media to bring awareness to his struggle by letting his fans know he was seeking help for a disorder he long battled with. He also spoke about his struggle in his music lyrics like other influential artists have (Lil Wayne, Jay-Z, Kanye West).

"Went through, deep depression when my mama passed/Suicide,

what kinda talk is that?"

_Kanye West

On a global scale, *PutMeOnIt.com*, a United Kingdom based entertainment website, conducted a campaign called, "It's OK to Not be OK." They did a series of interviews with global hip-hop artists who discussed their journey through depression. The site is no longer active after its 10-year run (2008-2018) of blogging, events, artist development, PR and more. However, the National Suicide Prevention Line opened the door for the It's OK to Not be OK campaign online to their You Matter platform, and in a 2016 article it highlighted how the service gives tips and words of hope to individuals who are suffering from mental illness.

Findings

Hip-hop has been found as a way for people to express themselves and deal with stress and other mental health disorders. In the article, "Hip-Hop Artists Have Been Writing About Mental Health for Decades," on *Huffington Post*, Allison Fox found that sixty million Americans suffer in some way with mental illness per year and each voice that comes forward reduces the stigma against it. In the case of artist Logic, according to the National Suicide Prevention Hotline, calls to the namesake phone number increased by 50 percent following the VMAs performance. (The

NSPH experienced a bump of 27 percent the day of the song's release back in April 2017). Many artists have focused on the doldrums of depression, hopelessness and contemplated ending it all on wax, whereas Logic's song presented an alternative, shifting the approach toward concern and encouragement. While this is just one example of what hip-hop can do in bringing awareness to communities, the results are endless.

Conclusion

A United Kingdom-based initiative Hip-Hop Psych, has been fighting the good fight of addressing mental health issues through hip-hop music. In an article titled, "A Hip-Hop State of Mind", co-founders Becky Inkster (neuroscientist at the Cambridge University's Department of Psychiatry) and Akeem Sule (consultant psychiatrist of the South Essex Partnership Trust) stated, that "Hip-hop music is rich with mental health references related to addiction, psychosis, conduct disorder, bipolar disorder, borderline personality disorder and so on, as well as multiple environmental risk factors and predisposing genetic and epigenetic risk factors." Hip-hop is opening the lines of communication amongst communities worldwide by making the conversation about mental health easier to have. Over time and with more research, the effects of hip-hop on mental health awareness and dealing with mental health disorders can show great benefits.

Allison Fox's article on *Huffington Post* also made affirmations by Jordan Simpson, a writer and slam poet, that "Hip-hop's conversation about mental health is nothing new... It's also a transformative process... These lyrics spread awareness."

"Pain don't hurt the same, I know
The lane I travel feels alone
But I'm moving 'til my legs give out
And I see my tears melt in the snow
But I don't wanna cry
I don't wanna cry anymore
I wanna feel alive
I don't even wanna die anymore
Oh I don't wanna
I don't wanna
I don't even wanna die anymore"

_'1-800-273-8255' by Logic

CHAPTER 7

PERFORMANCE ASSESSMENT & PROGRAM EVALUATION

Hip-hop as an adult became more about the lyrics and beat for me. Certain artists I respected and grew to love continued to thrive in their careers with great albums like Jay-Z, Kanye West, T.I., and Nas. As many of these artists moved on to veteran status in the hip-hop game, new upcoming artists began to play an important role in the music I listened as well. As you start to come into your own as an adult, you begin to face different obstacles in the real world like bills, politics, employment, and deeper relationships. Below is a list of albums and artists that heavily influenced me during my young adult, college days in Albany, New York.

2011	2012	2013	2014
Cole World: The Sideline Story–– J. Cole	*Unexpected Arrival––* Diggy Simmons	*Yeezus––* Kanye West	*2014 Forest Hills Drive––* J. Cole
Watch the Throne–– Jay-Z & Kanye West	*Pink Friday: Roman Reloaded––* Nicki Minaj	*Nothing Was the Same––* Drake	*The Pinkprint––* Nicki Minaj
Take Care–– Drake	Life is Good–– Nas	Born Sinner–– J. Cole	PartyNextDoor Two–– PartyNextDoor
	Good Kid, M.A.A.D. City–– Kendrick Lamar	Magne Carta... Holy Grail–– Jay-Z	Paperwork–– T.I.
	Dreams & Nightmares–– Meek Mill	PartyNextDoor––PartyNextDoor	

Hip-hop artists like Drake, Kendrick Lamar, Nicki Minaj, Meek Mill, and J. Cole were my top pick choices during the college years of independence and liberation. OG (for those who don't know, OG stands for original gangsta - a sign of respect in hip-hop culture), Nas reappeared on this scene with his *Life is Good* album in 2012. It was refreshing but also matched the tone I seemed to be riding along. The album highlighted the ups and downs of his life and his marriage that later ended in divorce. It was a way of dedicating and valuing the journey and beauty behind both the ups and downs of life. This is something later in life I came to understand after going through my own triumphs and struggles only to overcome all negativity and see the positive in every situation. GROWTH!

UNCONVENTIONAL, ICONIC & LYRICAL

'Lyrical - (of literature, art, or music) expressing the writer's emotions in an imaginative and beautiful way.' (Oxford Dictionary)

It is said that a lot of great things come from significant loses. Through darkness comes light, through fear comes love, and through pain comes triumph. Let's just say that during my darkest moments in college, I found light through various types of art, whether it be creating it or appreciating it. I chose the word lyrical to describe my tone for those years because my emotions were expressed in imaginative and beautiful ways through music, drawing, writing, poetry, dance, and more. With just a pencil, paper, and some background music, a photo of loved ones or nature could be recreated within the late-night hours into daybreak. My darkness (depression, anxiety, PTSD, and physical health issues), showed me the lights (my talents) within me and helped me begin to mold and grow them. However, my path is not the same and others.

In hip-hop, how effective an artist is in the culture is often measured by how successful their art is, and their contributions to the community. You never know how something is perceived until you evaluate the situation or receive feedback. This is the same for organizations when it comes to performance assessment and program evaluations.

Let's kick it off with the OG…

Job Analysis

Job analysis is a process that determines the duties and expectations of the job. Competency models are similar to job analysis because they are used to gather information from executives rather than lower level job employees about the job and the employee skills, however they usually start with defining competencies for executive jobs first and then work their way down the leadership and team lines. Job analysis involves the use of different techniques and assessments to break down job descriptions and person specifications. Job analysis is usually tailored to the Human Resource system for which it is created and conducted. A specific job analysis may be conducted to inform several HR systems, but this usually means including a broader range of descriptive traits and competencies that are being looked for in a potential candidate. The use of interviews, resumes, and other assessment tools can be used for job analysis and competencies. I keep using the term competency so let me give you a quick definition of what it is. A competency is a measurable pattern of knowledge, skills, abilities, behaviors, and other characteristics (KSAOs - the abbreviation) that an individual needs in order to perform work roles or occupational functions successfully.

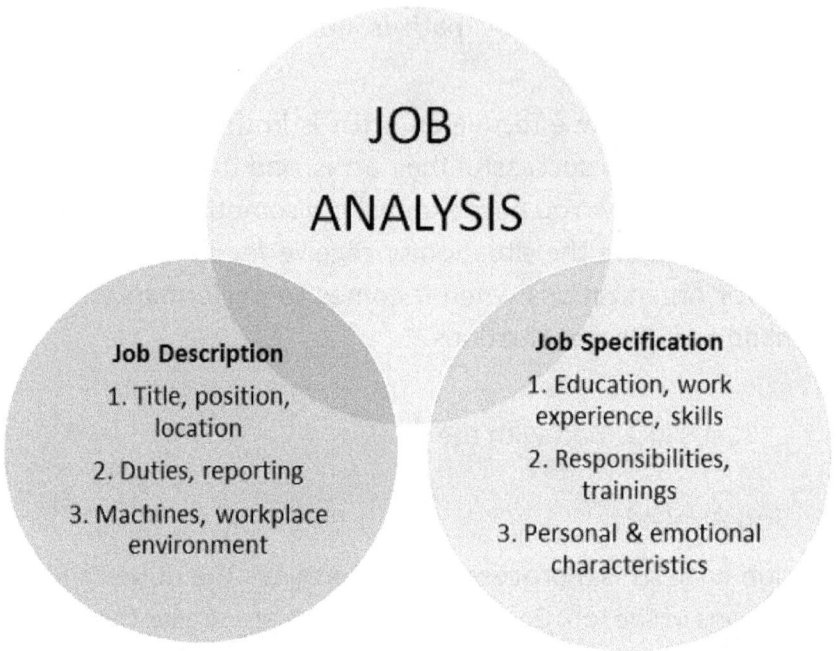

JOB ANALYSIS

Job Description
1. Title, position, location
2. Duties, reporting
3. Machines, workplace environment

Job Specification
1. Education, work experience, skills
2. Responsibilities, trainings
3. Personal & emotional characteristics

Steps of Job Analytics

Collect information about the job: position descriptions, subject matter expert input, performance standards, occupational studies.

List the tasks: list tasks and competencies required for a successful performance.

Identify the critical tasks: identify the importance of each task.

Identify the critical competencies: list and rate the importance of each competency, and apply cutoffs where needed.

The Lyrical OG

In terms of hip-hop, Nas is one of the OGs who laid the basis down for successful artists. Nas is a Queens, New York rapper, songwriter, record producer, actor, and entrepreneur who came on the scene in 1994 with his debut album *Illmatic*, an album that continues to be ranked as one of hip-hop's greatest albums. Known for its major influence on East Coast hip-hop, *Illmatic* went on to become platinum certified. Nas was also involved in a highly publicized feud between my idol Jay-Z during 2001-2005, something I clearly wasn't paying much attention to at the time... however, let's indulge in some history. The feud grew from a small snub between the two artists who did not come together to collaborate on Jay-Z's*Reasonable Doubt* album back in 1996. However, the highlight of this feud could easily be recorded when "Takeover" was released on Jay-Z's*Blueprint* that easily provoked Nas to deliver the notorious hit "Ether." Of course, it did not stop there between these two icons, because Jay Z followed up with his freestyle of Hot 97 radio show, "Supa Ugly," which followed with a lot of family backlash that resulted in both parties feeling the feud went too far. In 2005, the feud was brought to an epic end when Jay Z brought Nas out during his I Declare War tour. Both artistsperformed songs that poured more fire to the flame during the height of their feud. Nas went to later sign to Jay-Z's Def Jam Label after his deal with Columbia was over. A peaceful end in the hip-hop community.

In my childhood Jay-Z, Biggie, and Tupac were constantly on repeat. But Nas became significant in my life as I got older. His music influenced all ages to be great and the best they could be, just like his 2003 hit "I Can." His music always told stories and held many topics that were very big and relevant in the community. He is known to be one of hip-hop's greatest MCs with his conversational rap style and crazy lyrical technique. Now he is a tech entrepreneur, first investing in Rap Genius, Lyft, Dropbox, just to name a few.

I briefly touched upon Job Analysis and Competency modeling, so now let me give you some vital information on how these two differ. Traditional job analysis has been around for many years. The major purpose of a traditional job description is to outline the role and responsibilities of a position for supervisors and employees. They provide the structure for companies to set employee expectations and use a collection of data that managers and other sources to assess a job at that moment. The traditional job analysis describes all aspects of the job and the employee's performance.

On the other hand, competency modeling is fairly new. A competency-based job description expands on the job functions and responsibilities by adding skills, knowledge and behaviors necessary for success in a position. It is focused on the KSAOs (knowledge, skills, abilities, and other characteristics) needed for a job and uses qualitative techniques to assess a job. Competency modeling focuses primarily on the most important factors to be successful in a job further down the line. These competencies point out which type of employee would perform successfully in a job.

Performance Appraisal

Performance appraisal or evaluation refers to the assessment of individual employees (or volunteers) by management. Typically, performance appraisal involves a cycle of planning employee or teamwork objectives, assessing actual versus intended achievements, and communicating corrective action in advance of establishing future objectives. Performance appraisals involve the use of managerial ratings on each employee based on how well those objectives were met, and the areas in which the employee excelled or struggled.

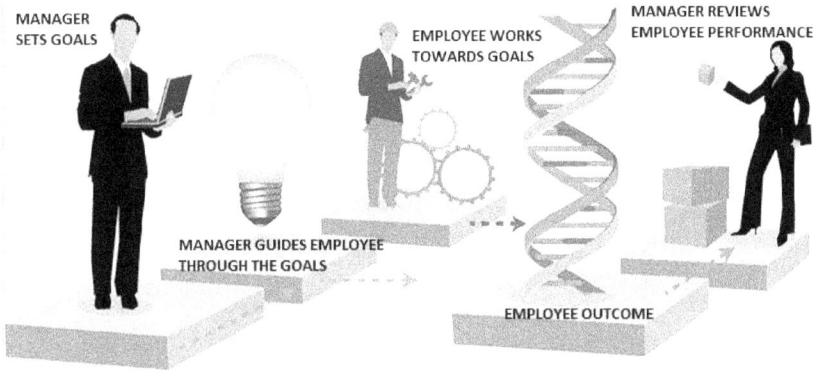

According to Marcus Buckingham (author, motivational speaker and consultant) and Ashley Goodall's *Harvard Business Review* article in 2015 "Reinventing Performance Management," they focused on three things for their performance management program: how to recognize performance, how to see it clearly, and how to fuel performance. They stated in the article, "We have three interlocking rituals to support them - the annual compensation, the quarterly or per-project performance snapshot, and the weekly check-in." Performance appraisals gauge their performance and a supervisors means of assessing and communicating job performance status to an employee, suggesting needed changes in behavior, attitude, skills or job knowledge. For supervisors, it is also used as a coaching tool and used to identify and deal with performance deficiencies.

In contrast, performance appraisals are used to demonstrate that businesses are operating and handling situations legally. Performance appraisals are one of the most powerful tools Human Resources can use to demonstrate that the organization has legitimate, non-discriminatory reasons for termination or other adverse action against an employee or unsuccessful job applicant. They provide the proper layout for expectations and consequences if problems with an employee arise and cannot be resolved.

Performance appraisal is seen to be effective on employee outcomes in positive workplace culture. Workplace culture has proven to moderate the relationship between performance appraisal process effectiveness in achieving self-reported performance, job satisfaction, and employee retention. A positive workplace culture—one in which employees have reason to believe that they are important to the organization—is the key feature in achieving the goals of performance appraisal. Observing performance appraisal in a positive setting improves the use of other performance appraisal tools in other organizations.

Finally, performance appraisals are only seen to be effective if they are tailored to the task and Key Performance Indicators. Different appraisal techniques are appropriate for different task types or jobs. It is not possible to achieve a perfectly accurate appraisal because of the nature of what is involved, it is still up to individual managers to create the environment necessary for the potential of appraisals to be released. To do this, managers should reward effective appraisals, provide opportunities for raters to observe the relevant behaviors to be rated, and make clear the exact purposes of the appraisal process.

Measuring Individual Differences

Individual differences are seen as important factors to predict the performance and behavior of employees in an organization. To examine and collect data on each individual's differences, assessments are implemented. Managers, supervisors, trainers, human resource professionals are conducting these assessments often under the guidance of practicing psychologists or at least using assessment platforms that were designed by psychologists and implemented on behalf of the company. These assessments originated during the First and Second World Wars by recruiting soldiers, they later evolved and are used for the following change:

Business Necessity

Individual Necessity

Research Necessity

What's Your Personality Type?

Use the questions on the outside of the chart to determine the four letters of your Myers-Briggs type.
For each pair of letters, choose the side that seems most natural to you, even if you don't agree with every description.

1. Are you outwardly or inwardly focused? If you:

- Could be described as talkative, outgoing
- Like to be in a fast-paced environment
- Tend to work out ideas with others, think out loud
- Enjoy being the center of attention

then you prefer

E
Extraversion

- Could be described as reserved, private
- Prefer a slower pace with time for contemplation
- Tend to think things through inside your head
- Would rather observe than be the center of attention

then you prefer

I
Introversion

2. How do you prefer to take in information? If you:

- Focus on the reality of how things are
- Pay attention to concrete facts and details
- Prefer ideas that have practical applications
- Like to describe things in a specific, literal way

then you prefer

S
Sensing

- Imagine the possibilities of how things could be
- Notice the big picture, see how everything connects
- Enjoy ideas and concepts for their own sake
- Like to describe things in a figurative, poetic way

then you prefer

N
Intuition

ISTJ	ISFJ	INFJ	INTJ
ISTP	ISFP	INFP	INTP
ESTP	ESFP	ENFP	ENTP
ESTJ	ESFJ	ENFJ	ENTJ

3. How do you prefer to make decisions? If you:

- Make decisions in an impersonal way, using logical reasoning
- Value justice, fairness
- Enjoy finding the flaws in an argument
- Could be described as reasonable, level-headed

then you prefer

T
Thinking

- Base your decisions on personal values and how your actions affect others
- Value harmony, forgiveness
- Like to please others and point out the best in people
- Could be described as warm, empathetic

then you prefer

F
Feeling

4. How do you prefer to live your outer life? If you:

- Prefer to have matters settled
- Think rules and deadlines should be respected
- Prefer to have detailed, step-by-step instructions
- Make plans, want to know what you're getting into

then you prefer

J
Judging

- Prefer to leave your options open
- See rules and deadlines as flexible
- Like to improvise and make things up as you go
- Are spontaneous, enjoy surprises and new situations

then you prefer

P
Perceiving

These assessments help companies know their employee's strengths and weaknesses and place them in the correct units. Additionally, these assessments can help individuals learn about themselves and help them evolve individually and as an employee.

The Myers Briggs Personality Inventory (MBTI) has been used to measure individual references for people in the workplace for many years. MBTI is an introspective self-report questionnaire used to indicate differing psychological preferences on each individual's unique perspective of the world they live in and how they make decisions. It is considered a personality preference tool that helps you understand who you are. Below are the five MBTI that help the workplace in many ways:

Appreciate differences
Improved teamwork
Improved relationships with your boss
Stronger customer insights
Recognize if you are in the right job

Training and coaching: Employers can use personality test results to develop leaders, such as executives and directors. Using this information, organizations can decide which leadership qualities to focus on more in their leadership development programs and the training needs of other individuals.

Work Environment: Learning the differences among these personality styles helps organizations develop programs and workplace rules that minimize conflict and improve communication among co-workers themselves and between workers and management.

The Lyrical Emotionalist

Drake is a Canadian rapper, singer, songwriter, record producer, actor and entrepreneur. I first came across him as an actor in a teen drama, *Degrassi: The Next Generation* that was out in the early 2000s. It wasn't until I entered college that Drake's music started to mean something in my life. He is more a blend of the rugged hip-hop and with a smooth R&B sound. He is known for his heartfelt lyrics and musical diversity, and his music crosses over many chart categories incorporating Caribbean influences, Canadian hip-hop elements, and pop. He opened up his own record label OVO Sound, which he used to discover and sign artists like PartyNextDoor, DVSN, Majid Jordan, and Kash Doll.

Drake is an artist who not only influenced me but the whole game in more ways than one. He was one of the first hip-hop artists to bring forth his personal life through his artwork so directly. I believe that being this raw with content has to, inevitably, connect with people. For what is real, is sacred. He had no gimmick as most artists do. He came forth with just his talent and life experiences and created timeless music. Another way he influenced the game was through his beat selection. His melodic flow, over-extraordinary sample selections have changed the way we hear and listen to rap music, and in turn changed the way it was made. It can easily be said that in the sense of business, his performance appraisals have influenced the way he continued to develop his music. The feedback he received from fans, fellow artists, and music empires fueled how he continued to perform. His individual differences have proven to work for him in his career and influences. He is a leader in the hip-hop game, and his individual differences are constantly being searched for in other artists. Many may come close to being similar to Drake, but no one can ever be Drake!

Recruitment, Selection, and Placement

According to Bernard O'Meara and Stanley Petzall book, *The Handbook of Strategic Recruitment and Selection: A Systems Approach*, staffing is important to an organization and can be critical in supporting their survival and growth. People are the main asset of any organization and it is the performance and commitment of staff members that makes a distinction between organizations. The recruitment, selection, and placement stages are all important in order to find an ideal candidate to fill a job vacancy, but also fulfill the duties and responsibilities of the job. The handbook states that recruitment refers to an organization's ability to:

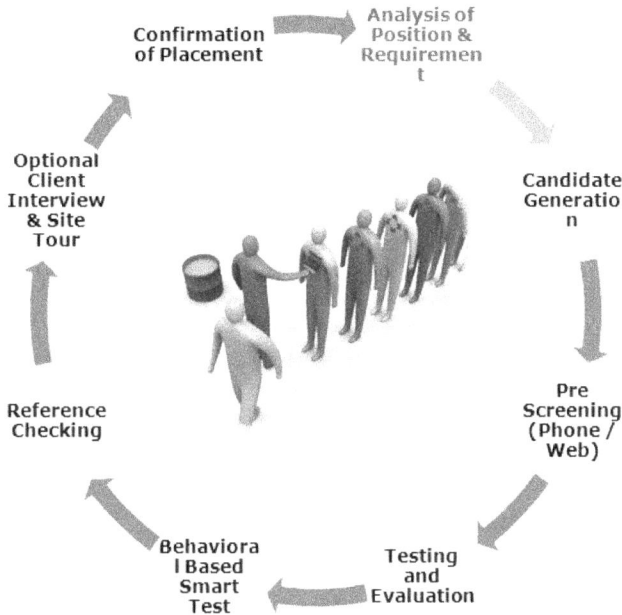

Attract a suitably qualified pool of applicants for a vacancy

Attract staff in a cost-effective manner

Attract staff in a timely manner so that appointments are made quickly

Provide a short-list of candidates to proceed to the selection phase

Following the recruitment phase is the selection phase. The selection phase allows the organization and applicants to acquire and pass on information to determine if they are suitable for one another. Many different tests and strategies are used in order to identify if the candidate is a right fit for the organization. These tests include aptitude, intelligence, and personality tests. However, each test must be used to focus on job-related criteria that is identified through job analysis. Multiple interviews may occur and sometimes candidates may be asked to demonstrate their skills in real life or a formulated situation. It is important to make sure that while going through the selection process, interviewers take into consideration the needs of the organization. Interviewers need to be able to align the organization's and the individual's short-, medium- and long-term needs.

The placement phase occurs once the organization has found a candidate who can handle the responsibilities of the job. There is a very rare time where organizations come across ideal candidates who fit both the job and the organization. The placement occurs when the candidate fits the job, performance over time, and the commitment to the company.

The Lyrical Ventriloquist

Nicki Minaj is a Queens, New York singer, songwriter, actress, rapper, and model. I first recognized her music when she released *Pink Friday* in 2010. Her style was bright and lively, very unique and based on the characters from her childhood that she metaphorically rapped about in her music. Over the years, her style has changed, and she has gained a big fan base, known as "The Barbz." She has had many endorsement deals and co-ownerships with top companies in cosmetics (M·A·C Cosmetics), liquor (MYX Fusions), electronics (Beats Electronics), and more (shareholder of Tidal).

She has acknowledged many of her major influences in music are Foxy Brown, Jay-Z, as well as Lil' Kim, whom she can be seen to have gained a lot of influence from. She has explored so many different genres of music in her albums outside of just hip-hop, and gained crossover charts success. Nicki Minaj has been compared to hip-hop artist Busta Rhymes as they share similarities of throwing their voices around in different directions. Nicki Minaj is one of hip-hop's highly awarded artist, gaining over 38 awards worldwide. In terms of business, she is the perfect example of a leader that can succeed in different genres, using an acrobatic vocal style of creating or portraying (recruiting/selecting/placing) certain characters in order to fit the job (genre/song) she is targeting.

When recruiting, selecting, and placing employees, there are a few things that organizations should avoid. I've composed six top mistakes that should be avoided.

Fail to prepare the interviewers: Make sure the proper questions are being asked and that each interviewer has a specific target they are assessing.

Not developing a suitable candidate pool: Have a suitable pool of candidates based on the needs of the organization and the roles to be filled.

Not having a list of appropriate questions to ask: Being prepared to have a standard set of questions can make it easier for interviewers to assess their candidates.

Not using multiple assessment tools: The use of just an interview to help decide on a candidate is not beneficial. The use of multiple assessment tools should be used.

Placing a candidate in an area they cannot excel in: Organizations look for individuals who can fit the job but also the organization. If the candidate's goals do not match the organization, it is not a good fit.

Failure to differentiate the critical job skills: If the job skills of a candidate do not match that of the candidate, they are not a good fit for the organization and you are setting them up for failure. The organization must know what they are looking for in the candidate that can benefit the organization and the customers.

Designing Training Programs

Designing training programs in organizations allows you to provide a development program for employees to better themselves as well as better the company. The first step in designing a program is by determining the overall goal you want to accomplish with the program. Do not overwhelm your employees with too many goals at once; learners are often better off to work towards at most two to four goals at a time. Next, you should determine the learning objectives and activities you want to use, that will ultimately help you accomplish your overall training and development goals. The following step is to develop and gather any materials that will be needed to perform the activities. Some materials may be made in order to fit the needs of the program. Training materials may not be available for the kind of you are looking to hold or in specific work fields. Many countries, however, have developed their own teaching materials.

After these core steps, the implementation of your training plan happens. In order to make sure your program is successful, thoroughly review all information. Check to see if any support is needed, and devise quick solutions in the event of minor issues occurring. Consider having a local training expert review the plan. Have someone check for errors and track your program to see if it is successfully accomplishing the goals set. Finally, the most crucial stage of them all, follow up after completion of your training program. Use the feedback from evaluations to adjust the content and methods of the training to meet participants' needs in the future better.

The Lyrical Improvisor

Meek Mill is a rapper and songwriter from Philadelphia. He originally started out as a battle rapper and then made the transition to mainstream music. He is currently signed to Mayback Music Group (MMG) under Rick Ross, a hip-hop artist with a lot of hit songs and collaborations. Meek Mill's mixtape series

Dreamchasers was my introduction to the Philly rapper. His influences stemmed from fellow Philly artists who played a part in my childhood and adult life, Will Smith and DJ Jazzy Jeff. All I can think about is watching the *Fresh Prince of Bel-Air* reruns in my pajamas and listening to Will Smith and DJ Jazzy Jeff's music, while eating ice cream in my dorm room. Their fun, laid back, happy vibe, on and off screen, was the perfect remedy for stress and long college nights. *Sigh What a time... * Meek Mill has that laid-back vibe in his flow as well, but his grit and rawness are on a different level. He constantly tailored his music to trap, hardcore rap, he did some of hip-hop love songs with Nicki Minaj (the hip-hop couple of the hour). He is best known for his mixtapes and feuds in the rap game, with the most publicized being his ongoing feud with Drake, that resulted in a few diss tracks leaving their followers in high suspense to see who would return with the hottest bars. The feud started to cool down due to the incarceration of Meek Mill, and during that time Drake campaigned for his release. The feud finally got put to rest after Drake invited Meek Mill onstage during his Aubrey and the Three Amigos tour with Migos in September 2018, where they both performed Meek Mill's hit song, "Dreams and Nightmares."

In the sense of business, Meek Mill is an improviser and creator, which is a very necessary trait in designing training programs. Training programs will always change over time depending on the needs of the organization or even the individual differences of the employees it is targeting. Being able to gather information, create new tools and solutions, and target a specific goal can be very difficult for many individuals, but if you are anything like Meek Mill, it's a no-brainer.

When planning a successful and effective training program there are three critical components that must be involved:

Learning objectives: It is important to create the learning objectives for the training program so there is a specific goal you are trying to obtain. You will learn that your employees are more actively engaged and learn more when they clearly understand how training relates to their jobs.

Involvement: Adults need to be a part of their training. A good training program has frequent built-in exercises that are both physically and mentally active. This involvement can include different activities in both small and large groups that the employees can do.

Proper Resources: Having the proper resources is crucial to implementing a successful program. This can come in the form of materials, financial assistance, leadership support.

Assessing Training Program Effectiveness

Training in any organization allows employees to build skills as individuals and as a team. However, each training program should be evaluated to see if it is effective, as these programs are costly and time-consuming. Also, if the training program is not effective, it will not reach the expectations or goals of the organization. Managers and organizations should focus on the effectiveness of training to ensure it delivers the expected organizational benefits.

In order to maximize the benefits of training, managers must closely monitor the training process. The training process consists of three phases: (1) needs assessment, (2) development and conduction of training, and (3) evaluation. Assessing the training program takes place during the evaluation phase The most well-known and used model for measuring the effectiveness of training programs was developed by Donald Kirkpatrick, Professor Emeritus at the University of Wisconsin and former president of the American Society for Training and Development, in the late 1950s. Kirkpatrick wrote a series of four articles for the magazine *ASTD* (the American Society of Training Directors) each covering one piece of the four levels which later became known as the Kirkpatrick Model. The Kirkpatrick model of measuring training effectiveness consists of four levels:

Reactions: how employees react to the training

Learning: how much the employees have advanced in skill, knowledge, and attitude

Behavior: how the skills learned are used every day

Results: how the training benefitted the organization

Kirkpatrick's Model

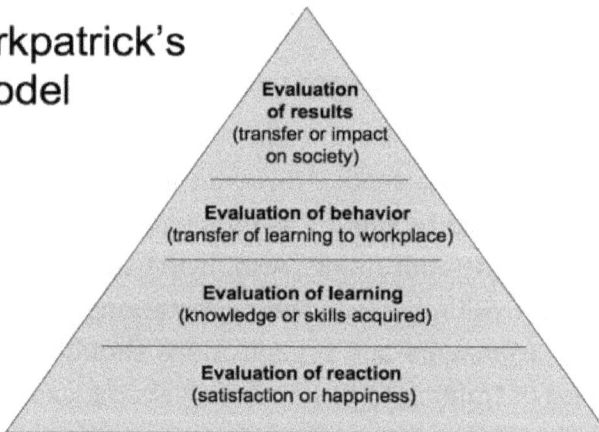

Evaluation
of results
(transfer or impact
on society)

Evaluation of behavior
(transfer of learning to workplace)

Evaluation of learning
(knowledge or skills acquired)

Evaluation of reaction
(satisfaction or happiness)

Kirkpatrick's (2006) hierarchy of evaluation.

Now, in order to gain information for an evaluation, there are a variety of ways in which it can be done: hardcopy and online quantitative reports; production and job records; interviews with participants, managers, peers, customers, suppliers and regulators; checklists and tests; direct observation; questionnaires, self-rating and multi-rating; and focus group sessions.

Designing Intervention Programs

Organizational Development interventions are structured programs that are designed to solve a problem, which will enable the organization to achieve the goal. They are main learning processes in the action phase of organization development initiated from the top of the organization and require employee participation and commitment. When designing an intervention program, there must be a strong leader to guide the program. Visionary leaders that work as change agents, developing a vision, and providing continuous and sustained support is of the greatest importance. Each program can target different parts of an organization. There are many different types of interventions: strategic, large-scale, techno-structural, management, and leadership development, team development and group processes, and individual/interpersonal process interventions.

There are nine steps to follow when strategically planning an intervention program:

Develop a mission: create a clear vision or focus on a specific problem that is being targeted to change.

Conduct critical analysis of the internal environment: The internal environment, refers to the nature of the organization itself, which is identified by certain characteristics including the organization's structure, culture, employee motivation, leadership, decision-making practices, communication patterns, and receptivity to change, to name a few. Focus on the characteristics of the organization, how each benefit or does not benefit the organization currently, and in the future, and how a change would occur, etc.

Conduct critical analysis of the external environment: Focus on how the environment aides or hinders organizational growth, and what factors of the environment influences the organization.

Prepare planning assumptions: The planning assumptions refer to the needs of the program and what would make it successful. The assumptions underlying the strategic planning process are important to the overall success of the strategic plan.

Develop a strategy: After careful assessment of the organization's position on the aforementioned factors or characteristics (e.g., the company's organizational structure, its culture, motivation of its members, leadership, decision-making strategies, communications, inclination toward change, and available resources), a decision is made on how to execute achieving the goal.

Communicate the strategy: Breakdown the strategy developed for execution, ensuring that all members have clarity on its purpose and the necessary tools/resources they will need to complete it.

Develop evaluation procedures: This includes the procedures for the implementation of the program and evaluations.

Implement strategy: Focus on the execution of the strategy, ensuring that it is completed to its entirety and aimed at improving its targeted goal.

Evaluate results: Go over the results and findings from the intervention program, and what could be used to improve results in the future.

Keep in mind that many critical components overlap in training and intervention programs. The three most critical components involved in the planning of an effective Organizational Development intervention are:

Needs and Resources: Analyze the needs of the organization and the environment internally and externally. Make sure that the organization has enough support and resources to plan and execute an Organizational Development intervention.

Develop and communicate strategy: Properly develop and communicate a structure on how the program will be implemented. This involves a lot of problem-solving and brainstorming.

Evaluation: Evaluate the results of the program to see if it has reached its targeted goal, and find ways to improve Organizational Development intervention for future use.

The Woke Lyrical Mind

Kendrick Lamar is a rapper and songwriter from Compton, California. He is a 12-time Grammy Award-winning artist known for his lyricism and performances. His strongest influences in the music industry are Tupac, Biggie, Jay-Z, and Eminem. Kendrick Lamar's artistic style and consistent controversial themes of music, both critical issues and commercial, have gotten him recognized by people in many different markets of business. He recently expanded his musical talents to create the soundtrack for the movie *Black Panther* which was released this year, 2018. This was a huge achievement to create the music for the first black superhero movie from Marvel (*WAKANDA FOREVER!!*) He can be named among other musical artists like himself who have produced soundtracks for Hollywood movies (Jay-Z with the *Great Gatsby*, Pharrell Williams with the *Despicable Me* franchise).

I came across Kendrick's music in 2012 with his *Good Kid, M.A.A.D. City* album while I was leaving campus late one night. I remember it pouring with rain and sitting inside of the Campus Center waiting for my car to warm up, a friend of mine came in the car and synced their phone to the car system and the first song I heard was "Money Trees." Instantly, I was hooked. *Good Kid, M.A.A.D. City* returned to the essence of hip-hop, which is storytelling. You can get lost in the tracks as they flow one into the other, complete with skits and interludes. It tells the story of a young Kendrick dealing with multiple issues, from trouble in his neighborhood to peer pressure to dealing with a girl. The storytelling he acquires holds so much realism - the danger, the bad choices, the close calls, and how normal it is for these events to occur. Heavy drums, horns, funk bass, and a different mix of sounds brought a groovy but modern sound to the album. From start to finish, you're on a ride with him and it's truly an all-encompassing experience. In terms of business, Kendrick Lamar fits the bill for designing intervention in the means of hip-hop. He uses the information from his internal and external environment to create what he feels can help bring awareness to hip-hop and its community. The evaluation of his artistry can be said to target and reach multiple facets within the hip-hop community, always showing a way for future projects to improve.

Evaluating Intervention Programs

The primary purpose of evaluating Organizational Development interventions is to prove the impact of interventions and/or to improve them for the future. Any evaluation phase has many advantages for the organization, the staff individually, as well as the teams, in the present day as well as the future. I will go over a nine-step practical guideline on how to plan, organize, implement, and report the evaluation of Organizational Development interventions effectively and efficiently (please remember that many key components of training and intervention programs, and their evaluation processes overlap):

Planning the OD evaluation: Identify what the needs of the organization are and how to handle them before the intervention.

Identifying key stakeholders and decision-makers: Identify and recognize those who have the final authority to judge the effects of, as well as make decisions regarding the Organizational Development interventions.

Determining evaluators and evaluation criteria: Identify what characteristics to focus on and what tools to use to evaluate them.

Scanning for internal and external relevant information: Search for any critical internal and external information related to the organization to understand the unique organizational characteristics and any significant internal and/or external events (e.g., massive layoffs, Mergers and Acquisitions, or law/regulation changes in labor union), which may affect or distort the results of the evaluation.

Selecting data collection methods: Choose which data collection method is best suited for the intervention.

Collecting data: Acquire information from the data collection method selected as well as any other information that may be relevant to the intervention.

Analyzing data: Examine the data that was acquired and use that data to transform the information to support and/or determine intervention goals.

Evaluate OD interventions: Use quantitative data analysis to focus on numerical data and qualitative data analysis to focus on subjective and intangible data.

Report the evaluation findings: These evaluation findings are used to improve future programs as well as sustain positive outcomes. Reporting the results are important to get them into the hands of stakeholders and organizational heads, that can use them for future research or general knowledge.

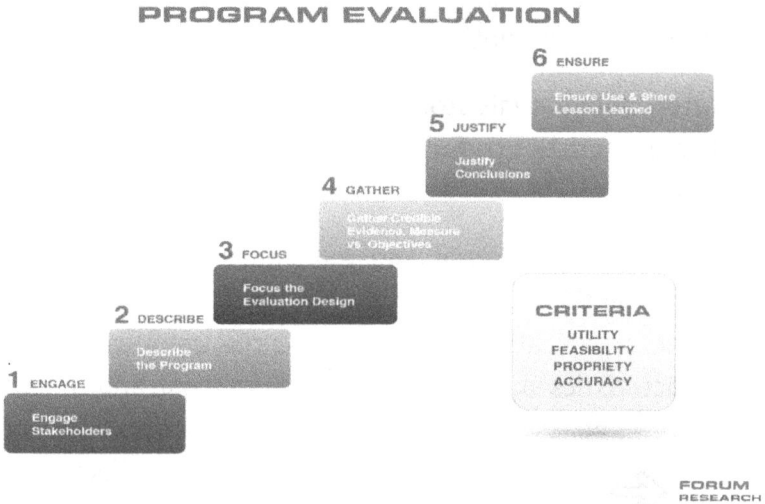

PROGRAM EVALUATION

6 ENSURE — Ensure Use & Share Lesson Learned

5 JUSTIFY — Justify Conclusions

4 GATHER — Gather Credible Evidence, Measure vs. Objectives

3 FOCUS — Focus the Evaluation Design

2 DESCRIBE — Describe the Program

1 ENGAGE — Engage Stakeholders

CRITERIA
UTILITY
FEASIBILITY
PROPRIETY
ACCURACY

FORUM RESEARCH

With these steps, thinking about the Organizational Development intervention evaluation is built into the change process at the beginning instead of it being an afterthought—something to be done at the end. As such, it can help to focus decision-makers on what results they really wish to achieve from a change effort by getting them to consider, and agree on, how to measure results.

The Lyrical Soul

J. Cole is a hip-hop recording artist and record producer from North Carolina, who made his debut in 2011 with *Cole World: The Sideline Story*, which later became a certified platinum album just like all four of his other albums that were later released. He took to the stage discussing real-life issues that people go through on a day-to-day basis just like Drake did, rapping about relationship issues, family, fame, and being successful, or lack thereof. His albums are always easy to listen to from beginning to end with its mellow vibe, his carefree persona, and realism at its highest peak. It can easily give you a feeling you are on a world ride with him. His *2014 Forest Hills Drive* album took fans and the hip-hop community by surprise in that it is an album that went double platinum with no features from other artists and won Album of the Year at the 2015 BET Hip-Hop Awards, and Top Rap Album at the 2015 Billboard Music Awards. He also went onto creating his record label, Dreamville Records, using his talents as a producer to assist other artists such as Kendrick Lamar and Janet Jackson. J Cole is one of many artists to leave a mark on his community through his non-profit organization The Dreamville Foundation, whose focus is on bridging the gap between the world of opportunity and the urban youth.

In terms of business, J. Cole embodies the nature of evaluating the intended outcome of interventions in the beginning stages. He uses the information from his past experiences and the current environment to tailor into his music the goals he would like to see from the youth and the world. His most recent album *KOD*, which was released in April of 2018, touches many topics including drug abuse, addiction, depression, greed, African-American culture, and taxation in the United States. He has a way of turning sad and negative situations into teaching tools, with *KOD* shedding concern and compassion to the journey of life that may not be warned by others. Since joining his mentor Jay-Z at Roc Nation, J. Cole has gone on to acquire more business acumen, and is now a shareholder of Tidal. He has such a humbling and laid-back persona that he constantly portrays during his performances and in his music. His music has touched the lives of many people by speaking the truth and encouraging change. His *2014 Forest Hill Drive* was the album I listened to during my graduating year. It got me through a lot of rough nights and spoke to me in ways that music is now lacking. Some of his best lines for motivation come from this album. So I will do you one better... Just a little sample of "The Lyrical Soul," "03' Adolescence," and "Love Yourz."

"To look behind and say,
Look where I came
Look how far I done came
They say that dreams come true
And when they do,
that there's a beautiful thing."

-J. Cole, Intro 2014 Forest Hill Drive

"Things change, rearrange, or so do I
It ain't' always for the better, dawg, I can't' lie
I get high 'cause the lows can be so cold
I might bend a little bit but I don't' fold"

-J. Cole, "03' Adolescence"

"It's beauty in the struggle, ugliness in the success
Hear my words or listen to my signal of distress
I grew up in the city and though sometimes we had less
Compared to some of my niggas down the block,
man, we were blessed."

-J. Cole, "Love Yourz"

Performance Assessment & Program Evaluation:

The BET Hip-Hop Awards

The BET Hip-Hop Awards is an annual award show acknowledging members of the hip-hop community and their success during the year, showcasing different hip-hop producers, performers, and music video directors. Many of the hottest artists are asked to perform their hitmakers of the year or pay tribute to great artists who left an impact on the culture and community of hip-hop. In true hip-hop form, cyphers are aired throughout the show displaying veteran and upcoming underground artists. A myriad of entertainers grace the stage as hosts of the evening for this sought-afteraffair.

The categories for these awards cover different contents of hip-hop. Some of these categories include: Lyricist of the Year, Producer of the Year, Hot Ticket Performer, Best New Hip-Hop Artist, Made-You-Look Award (Best Hip-Hop Style), Best Collaboration, Duo or Group, Best Hip-Hop Video, Best Mixtape, Best Hip-Hop Online Site/App, and Impact Track. Like any performance assessment in organizations, these awards are given after each artists' career has been assessed over the year. BET sends out electronic ballots and voters nominate categories who they think should be award nominees. These are collated by an organization called Yangaroo, that narrow the data to the top five nominees in each category, and send that list back out to a voting academy made up of about 500 people from the music industry, media, and blogger communities to vote on the winners.

After these awards are given, fans conduct an analysis of their own, indirectly, on many different social media platforms (Twitter, Instagram, Facebook, and Snapchat). With the following the hip-hop community has, this feedback comes from millions of people. The BET Hip-Hop Awards 2017 ceremony averaged 1.49 million overall viewers based on live and same-day data posted by Showbuzz Daily, an organization that provides up-to-the-minute predictions and analysis on viewership. They rate how they feel the award show transpired, the performances, best and worst dressed, and give their opinions on who they felt should have won the awards and other topics. BET has even opened categories that allow the public to vote on the winner. In terms of the show, producers and creators of the BET Awards show take the feedback received from the show's airing and use the information to inform show creation for the following year. The BET Hip-Hop Awards is one of many award shows (Billboard Awards, BET Awards, MTV Awards, Grammys, etc.) that showcase hip-hop in its many forms.

The BET Hip-Hop Awards is not just an assessment of different individuals in the hip-hop community, but also a tool to bring acknowledgment to different people and different issues. Many people in the hip-hop community use the award ceremony platform to raise awareness on social issues, as well as give motivation and hope to fans and fellow artists. When hip-hop veteran, Snoop Dogg received the "I Am Hip-Hop" award at the 2016 BET Hip-Hop Awards, he left great words for fellow artists that embodied the true positive psychology nature and urged them to stay true to themselves.

"Hip-hop was created many years ago and it's grown, and it's taken people to so many places. You've gotta understand as a young MC, as a young artist, you've gotta always be who you are because at the end of the day, you've gotta live with who you are."

- Snoop Dogg, BET Awards, 2016

That's Uncle Snoop for you.

CHAPTER 8

OCCUPATIONAL HEALTH PSYCHOLOGY

I magine a kid growing up taking long drives down south. Mainly going to visit your grandparents for summer vacation, but unbeknownst to you, it was the three-month span where your parents gained freedom from parenting and from you...

OOOOO HOW THE TABLES HAVE TURNED!!

Nobody warned them?! When their kids have kids, they become the designated vacation spot, EVERY WEEK!! THE SUMMER SPOT IS YEAR-ROUND... IT'S LIT!

Ok ok... back to the flashback

As you are in the van driving down south the Fugees are playing...

> *"Strumming my pain with his fingers*
> *Singing my life with his words*
> *Killing me softly with his song*
> *Killing me softly with his song*
> *Telling my whole life with his words*
> *Killing me softly with his song"*
> _"Killing Me Softly" by Fugees

Of course, by the breakdown part, you're singing it at the top of your lungs like your Lauryn Hill…and by the end of the song you're getting taught how to rap your home phone number…

…Memories

Now where am I going with this? Lauryn Hill and the Fugees were always in my life but like other great artists they didn't impact my life until much later. They, as a group, targeted issues in society and brought awareness to many people in the early 1990s into the 2000s. From the beginning, with hip-hop and my family upbringing, I had a strong understanding about the benefits people can gain from having support from others around them. The hip-hop community has been very big in its efforts to bring awareness or aid to others through many different philanthropic measures. These positive efforts embody what you can see in Occupational Health Psychology.

"Just because a person smiles all the time, doesn't mean their life is perfect. That smile is a symbol of hope and strength." -Unknown Author

Theories and Concepts of Organization Health Psychology

Organizational/Occupational Health Psychology has opened the doors for many different theories and concepts to form a focus on the health, safety, well-being, and motivation of employees.

Theories

Herzberg's Two Factor Theory: Fredrick Herzberg was an American psychologist who is famous for introducing job enrichment and the Motivator-Hygiene theory known as Herzberg's Two Factor Theory. In Herzberg's two factor theory, he focuses on factors that affect motivation: hygiene factors and motivators. Hygiene factors determine dissatisfaction, and motivators determine satisfaction. The two scales are independent. Motivators consist of factors like career progression, responsibility, recognition, etc. Hygiene factors are factors like salary, benefits, work conditions, security, etc. This theory implies that you must work on improving both motivator factors and hygiene factors in order to produce a productive workforce and happy morale.

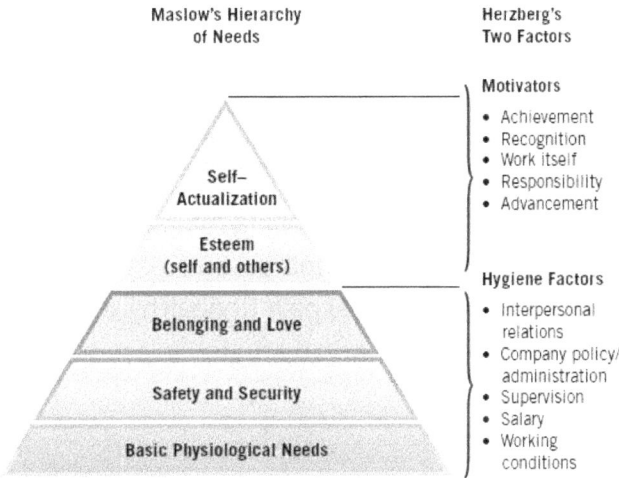

Maslow's Hierarchy of Needs | Herzberg's Two Factors

Self–Actualization

Esteem (self and others)

Belonging and Love

Safety and Security

Basic Physiological Needs

Motivators
- Achievement
- Recognition
- Work itself
- Responsibility
- Advancement

Hygiene Factors
- Interpersonal relations
- Company policy/ administration
- Supervision
- Salary
- Working conditions

Maslow's Hierarchy of Needs: Abraham Maslow was an American psychologist who is best known for creating Maslow's Hierarchy of Needs. This theory states that an individuals' most basic needs must be met before they become motivated to achieve higher level needs. The levels of the hierarchy from bottom to top are physiological, safety, love/belonging, esteem, and self-actualization. Just like Herzberg's two-factor theory and the hygiene factors, the physiological and safety factors control dissatisfaction and when an employee is not satisfied in those areas, they cannot provide their best work output. In order to reach the highest level of motivation (self-actualization, esteem, love/belonging) you must obtain the lower levels first (physiological and safety).

Cognitive Evaluation Theory:Similar to Herzberg's two-factor theory, there are two motivation systems focused on: intrinsic and extrinsic motivators. Intrinsic motivators are achievement motivators that come from the actual performance of the task or job, which consists of factors like achievement, responsibility, and competence. Extrinsic motivators are motivators that come from a person's environment, controlled by others, which consists of factors like pay, promotion, feedback, working conditions. The intrinsic needs are seen higher and less of an immediate priority for satisfaction, which is similar to that of Maslow's hierarchy of needs. Another similarity to Maslow in this theory is that the extrinsic motivators can have major negative effects on intrinsic motivators if they are negatively controlled by others. In the workplace this can take the form of a controlling manager who takes advantage of how they speak to employees or pay employees. Negative feedback, lack or unequal pay, unhealthy work environment can have a negative effect on an employee's work performance.

Concepts

Occupational Health Psychology also provides different concepts that are used or recognized in the workplace. Two concepts and two models that are prevalent in OHP are the concept of work engagement, the concept of psychological contracts, the Demand-Control-Support Model, and the Effort Reward Imbalance model. Each concept and model differ from each other but still focus on the important aspects of a healthy work environment, safety, and employee well-being.

The concept of work engagement focuses on strong work identification and energy. Work engagement is an independent, distinct concept that is typically related negatively to burnout. However, contrary to those who suffer from burnout, employees who are engaged in their work have a sense of energetic and effective connection with their work. Instead of looking at their work as stressful and demanding they look upon it as challenging. Organizations want to make sure they are hiring people who are engaged in their job and are ultimately enjoying it. Unhappy employees can lead to health risks, and negative effects on job performance and the environment.

The concept of psychological contracts focuses on the thought process and interpretation of employees. A psychological contract is considered "a deal in the mind," an individual's understanding of what they owe an employer and what they can expect in return from that employer. Often it is seen as unwritten rules, but comes from what's written in the handbook, what the incentives are, and so forth. Organizations need to ensure policies and protocols for the safety of their employees. This can come in forms of physical safety rules to benefits and job security.

The Demand-Control-Support Model highlights well-being. Workplace stress is a result of how demanding a person's job is and how much control and supports the person has. When employees are in a high demand job with low control and low support or isolation, it can have a negative effect on employee well-being. Support has been shown to moderate the negative impact of stress/strain on well-being.

The Effort Reward Imbalance Model highlights the interplay between job-related psychological effort and rewards, and individual commitment as a predictor of stress/strain. It is the belief that an imbalance between (high) efforts and (low) rewards leads to (sustained) strain reactions. The ERI uses the variables of effort, reward, and overcommitment scores to measure strain/stress in the workplace.

Stand Up

Ludacris is a Grammy award-winning rapper and actor based in Atlanta, Georgia. He is known as one of the first influential "Dirty South" rappers (along with Big Boi and André 3000 of the rap duo Outkast) to take mainstream by storm in the early 2000s. Ludacris' philanthropic efforts are linked to groups such as Artists for Peace and Justice, Stand Up to Cancer, and the Ludacris Foundation. Artists for Peace and Justice (APJ) encourages peace and social justice, working to alleviate poverty around the world, with their immediate efforts serving the poorest communities in Haiti. Stand Up to Cancer (SU2C) focuses on raising funds to bring awareness and accelerate cancer research to develop new breakthrough therapies and save lives. The Ludacris Foundation inspires youth of all ages through education, uplifting families and communities, and fostering economic growth. It has been named one of the Top 20 "Leading Philanthropy Foundations" by *Black Enterprise* magazine, featured in *The Robb Report's Worth* magazine, as well as *The Chronicles of Philanthropy* (a Newspaper that reports on the non-profit world) for outstanding efforts provided to urban communities. Ludacris strives to help others and has continued to do so over the years by devoting himself to many causes including cancer research, the environment, at-risk youth, AIDS, human trafficking, poverty, and literacy. In 2009, when flooding hit Atlanta, leaving many schools and homes underwater, he donated to recovery efforts and handed out more than 500 coats to students. After one of the strongest tropical cyclones in 2013, Typhoon Haiyan, Ludacris made a generous donation to the United Nations agency scurrying to feed the battered Philippines. On a smaller, but also impactful scale, Ludacris helped to build a playground for Venetian Hills Elementary School after learning they had gone years without one.

The Changing Nature of Work

The changing nature of work has influenced the emergence of Occupational Health Psychology. The need for occupational health psychology has emerged because of evolution needs like job security, benefits, work conditions and safety. According to the National Research Council, analysts see changes in the nature of work as more gradual and evolutionary. And that society is experiencing increases and, in many ways, expect adaptations to shift in demography, technology, markets, organizational structures, and employment practices.

The nature of work has changed in its structure, content, and process. In the past, work was based on employee production in a product-based industry. Work is now more cognitively complex, team-based, dependent on social skills, and on the knowledge of technology, time-sensitive, and mobile. In today's nature of work, there are increasing pressures on organizations to be more competitive, agile, and customer-focused.

The changes in workforce stemmed from communication and technology breakthroughs. For the organization to be successful the demands of the employee changed. Technology has opened the doors for organizations to spread. More non-core job functions, such as IT, human resources, accounting, purchasing, and corporate real estate, are being outsourced. This causes the downsizing of central offices, leaving employment open to contractors and smaller and cheaper distributors. The remaining functions are being distributed nationally and globally, mainly driven by lower labor costs in other regions, accessibility to internal or external customers, and access to talents and skills not available in the local area. If employees do not have the required skill or technological competence for the job, they are no longer of use.

Employers are expected to be technologically competent, team-oriented, and sociable in today's work. The workforce composition has changed from traditional employee-employer relationships, to organizations hiring contract employees (independent contractors, temporary workers, and day laborers). Although there are changes, workers continue to prove their importance in the workplace, unfortunately they are still not offered what they deserve. According to Thomas Perez, U.S. Secretary of Labor, in a *Monthly Labor Review* article, "From 1973 to 2013, productivity has continued to rise (an increase of 74.4 percent), while hourly compensation for the typical worker has virtually flattened (up only 9.2 percent)."

There has also been a change in the socio-demographics of working families, as well as social or cultural trends. Some of the changes in the socio-demographic of working families and social or cultural trends that have posed greater challenges in employees being productive members of an organization and are seen in the number of employees who are married or living with their children, the number of middle age individuals in the workforce, and the level of education in which each employee has.

According to reports made by Robert Lerman and Stefanie Schmidt on the U.S. Labor Market, found on the Department of

Labor website, "to some extent, it is changes in employment opportunities that cause changes in marriage and family formation patterns and not the other way around." It is seen that labor force participation rates are higher amongst unmarried men, and labor market outcomes are better amongst men living with at least one of their children. Employees with children or families may pose challenges to employee's abilities to function positively at work if there are stressors going on at home and they overlap at work. These employees need to be able to balance their attention at work and at home in case of emergencies do happen.

Lerman and Schmidt affirmed that the declining numbers of 25-34-year old's, together with their changing ethnic mix, may portend shortfalls in key professional areas. Over the next decade, instead of having nearly all increases in employment coming from the 25-54-year old's, fewer than one in three (31 percent) of the added workers will be in this category. These declines in prime age workers will cause a change in the type of experience and knowledge present at the workforce. This will leave the workforce dependent on younger employees who have a different work ethic than the older employees who have more experience than recent training. It can cause conflict amongst employees with communication due to the age difference and different understandings. According to Lerman and Schmidt "Labor markets are generating jobs with higher skill requirements, but taking advantage of these opportunities requires expanded training opportunities, especially among older workers trying to avoid the effects of obsolescence." This plays a role on who the organizations are looking to hire or keep at the job. This can cause a stressor on the employee, whether they can meet the new demands or the stressor on their security at the company. The training that these organizations may offer are not really tailored to training less educated workers, so this will cause a strain on the training system.

Take a Chance

Chance the Rapper is a Grammy award-winning rapper, singer, songwriter, record producer, and actor from Chicago, Illinois. He came on the scene as an independent rapper who refused to sign to any record label in order to preserve his sound and the content of which he wanted to make music. Chance the Rapper has won over 13 awards including two BET Awards, two BET Hip-Hop Awards, as well as three Grammys for Best New Artist, Best Rap Album, and Best Rap Performance. Chance made history by being the first artist to win a Grammy with a project that was released exclusively through streaming platforms and by being the first black hip-hop artist to win Best New Artist since Lauryn Hill in 1999. His philanthropic efforts can be seen through his charity, SocialWorks, which aims to empower youth in Chicago through arts, education, and civic engagement while fostering leadership, accessibility, and positivity. Chance the Rapper is noted for giving $1 million to Chicago schools with extra assistance from his charity to donate $10,000 for every $100,000 raised. He also works on combatting gun violence in his hometown, raises money to put coats on kids backs, brings technology upgrades to schools, among other endeavors. In terms of business, Chance aims to impact how we implement change (change in the nature of work) within our community through empowerment, motivation and providing the proper tools (e.g. technology, leadership) necessary for youth to succeed.

STAND UP FOR ERGONOMICS:
THE ERGONOMIC OFFICE

Job design lays the foundation for how a job is operated and the tools or safety precautions implemented in order to make sure the job is operated safely. There are five job components that increase the motivating potential of a job: skill variety, task identity, task significance, autonomy, and feedback. When employees are given feedback about their effective performance or how they made an impact, can boost their confidence. When an employee is given the proper resources to do their job and the support needed if injured while on the job, they feel more secure and trust their organization. Ergonomics is also crucial and seen in many workplaces because it provides tools and resources that will allow an employee to complete a job while alleviating or preventing workplace stressors, illnesses, injuries, and deaths.

Ergonomics is simply fitting the workplace to the worker. Construction, manufacturing, healthcare, transportation are some examples of organizations that practice ergonomics. Montana State Fund, a company that partners with employers and their employees to care for those injured on the job and advocate for a culture of workplace safety, stated three basic ergonomics that can be seen in any workplace and help reduce stressors. Proper posture is one ergonomic.

Maintaining the proper posture can help reduce fatigue, eliminate strains, and reduce stress on ligaments and joints. Managing forces is also very important. Limiting the load, you are moving, lifting, or pulling is key to not strain your body. If the task is too difficult or heavy, ask for some assistance. Finally, many jobs require excessive repetitive motions and the effects can cause physical strains. If you're constantly sitting or standing, stretch and move to change and realign your body.

New technologies have enhanced the field of ergonomics because it has given employees more ways to stay safe on the job, as well as reduce stress and strains on their bodies. Some technology has even replaced the risk of the employee on the worksite where they can operate the technology remotely. Aside from technology, job design, and ergonomics, there are organizations that are put in place to ensure the safety and well-being of the employees.

Organizations such as the federal Occupational Safety and Health Administration (OSHA) and the National Institute for Occupational Safety and Health (NIOSH) affect work and job design because they provide research, recommendations, and mandates that prevent or protect work-related injuries and illnesses. If organizations do not have job sites permitted or approved by OSHA and NIOSH to operate, the organization can be shut down until all permits are updated and violations paid off. On the other hand, OSHA and NIOSH protect organizations as well. For certain employees to be considered eligible to work on certain jobs, they must be certified from training courses provided by OSHA and NIOSH.

Bad Boy for Life

It's P. Diddy... That's all I'm going to say about the type of man he is in hip-hop. Now in his philanthropic efforts... Those are just as endless and amazing as his career. He has always given back to his community in multiple ways. When the Boys & Girls Club of Harlem was going bankrupt, he pulled them from insolvency with a $60,000 donation. He raised $2 million for children's charities by running the New York Marathon, as well as gave a $1 million donation to his alma mater, Howard University, for business scholarship and internships. He supports many groups like the Jackie Robinson Foundation, Tony Hawk Foundation, and The Prince's Trust. The Jackie Robinson Foundation (JRF) is a national not-for-profit organization that addresses the achievement gap in higher education. The Tony Hawk Foundation supports disadvantaged communities and at-risk children by being the only national grant-writing organization focused on the development of safe, quality public skateparks. The Prince's Trust is a United Kingdom charity that aids and supports 11 to 30-year-olds who are unemployed and/or struggling at school. He also sits on the board of the Hip-Hop Action Summit and has been quick to "Blow a Check" on a variety of charities, including the Breast Cancer Research Foundation, Network for Teaching Entrepreneurship and the i.am Scholarship Foundation. After Hurricane Sandy in 2012, P. Diddy co-hosted the Superstars for Sandy Relief party, which raised $524,742. In relations to business, P. Diddy is providing tools (scholarships, internships) for the workplace (schools, environment) to fit the worker (student, members of the community).

Work-Related Stress

Job stress is explained as the unfortunate physical and mental reactions that appear when the job demands do not match with the abilities, skills, or requirements of the employee. Bad health and injury can result from job stress. Job stressors can come in many forms. There are three main common types of stressors: calamitous occurrences, major transitions, and daily problems. Different stressors that challenge employees in the workplace can come in two forms, physical stressors and psychosocial stressors.

Physical stressors can come from just about any job that requires a lot of repetitive movements, sitting or standing, lifting, pushing, etc. The prolong repetitive movements can cause wear and tear on the body, causing injury or pain. In many occupational fields, employees may be exposed to a variety of physical stressors that can cause illness, diseases, injuries, or death. The impact of these Occupational Health diseases or injuries on the productivity, sustainability, and performance of organizations is noteworthy. When your employees are in a negative state of health (emotionally, mentally, and/or physically) it poses a problem on their attendance like excessive absenteeism, work productivity, working below capacity, inefficiencies, output problems, and organizational interactions like morale issues.

Psychosocial stress can include anything that converts to a perceived threat to your social status, social esteem, respect, and/or acceptance within a group; threat to your self-worth, or a threat that you feel you have no control over. Both

physical and psychosocial stressors can have physiological, mental, and emotional responses in individuals. These stressors may affect individuals differently because each individual perceives stress in their own way. One of your employees may benefit from workplace pressure and work harder to prove their worth and value, whereas another employee may buckle under pressure and have reactions like panic attacks or excessive sweating.

However, psychosocial stress could benefit productivity and organizational success when your employees have positive stressors like healthy organizational competition, compete to be more successful than another organization. This stress would push your employees to work at their best because their organizational status may be at stake. When psychosocial stress triggers a stress response, the body releases a group of stress hormones including cortisol, epinephrine (or adrenaline) and dopamine, which will lead to a burst of energy as well as other changes within the body. However, just like any other kind of stress these effects can have longer negative effects on the body if they are not managed.

One Mic

Nas has taken to his philanthropic efforts in several ways, but especially through the arts. He supports groups like UNICEF, Save the Music Foundation, and Saving Our Daughters. Saving Our Daughters is an organization which works with girls from multicultural backgrounds through theater, film, culinary, and literacy to help them to overcome obstacles they may face growing up:

bullying (cyber, gossip, face-to-face), dating abuse, domestic violence, and other esteem slayers. Nas is highly recognized for his aide to a widower of eight who lost his home in a fire after he launched a Tilt campaign that raised almost $65,000 for Stanley Young's housing. As I stated above, Nas does his work through the arts, through personal work or creating opportunities for others through the arts. During Art Basel in 2011, he pushed the envelope by painting during his set at Miami's Ricochet Bar & Lounge. He later sold his first-ever masterpiece at an impromptu auction for $14,000, which he donated to a children's cancer charity. Now, how does this correlate with business? Stress has both negative and positive effects. In the case of Nas, he pushes initiatives that aid negative stressful situations to turn them into beautiful outcomes. For instance, he personally took on the task of adding the painting feature to his performance (healthy positive psychosocial stress) and turned it into a positive contribution to a charity.

Work/Life Balance

The importance of work-life balance for today's employees is necessary for organizations and the environment. Nigel Marsh, management consultant, communications specialist, author, and entrepreneur, argued that individuals need to be realistic with their situation and themselves and take control and responsibility of their lives. Elongate the time frame in which life is balanced and be realistic with the timeframe chosen to find and maintain this balance. Nigel Marsh also believes balance should be included in all areas of an individual's life: intellectual, emotional, spiritual, and physical. In his 2011 TED Talk "How to Make Work-Life Balance Work," he stated, "If you don't design your life, someone else will, and you may not like it."

Globalization and the competitive nature of business have created lean organizations with cultures that reward people who work unusually hard, spend longer hours at work, and are connected to the organization 24/7 via information, and communication technologies (e.g., computers, telephones). With the pressures on the organization to globalize and expand, as well as the pressures on employees who are being replaced by technology to complete jobs, the pressure on employees to overwork themselves creates challenges to achieve good work/life balance.

An imbalance of employees' work and personal obligations can have a lot of negative effects on employees and organizational health. If you don't allow yourself enough personal time, you'll become too burned out to appreciate any part of your life. Employees can start to develop different illnesses and diseases, and it can also cause a strain on their home life.

To achieve work/life balance, introduce EAPs or EWPs to the workplace.

Employee Wellness Programs: EWPs are designed and integrated in the workplace in a way that employees can reduce the risk of diseases through programs and lead healthier lives. EWPs are available to all employees and can involve providing gym memberships, transportation opportunities, healthy lunches or snacks, or incentives as such to promote a healthy lifestyle.

Employee Assistance Programs: EAPs are worksite-based programs that address organizational and individual issues that impact the work environment and employee productivity. EAPs typically provide an employee assessment on personal, emotional, family, and practical problems. EAPs are commonly seen as a part of an employee wellness program. These assistance programs are available to all employees but are usually given on a confidential basis to employees who are experiencing problems that affect their work attendance or productivity based on an employee request or managerial referral.

Cole World

J. Cole started The Dreamville Foundation which provides programs and events that inspire, encourage, and support urban youth. The annual Dreamville Weekend focuses on uplifting the Fayetteville community with an appreciation dinner, a career panel of African-American professionals and events honoring community leaders. It's all part of the effort to help urban youth "have a dream, believe in their dream, and achieve their dream." He provided students with the necessary supplies needed for school and has also opened the doors of a transitional home for single mothers. Before the beginning of the 2013 school year, J. Cole kicked off a tradition of donating school supplies – including backpacks, notebooks and pens. He also announced that his old Fayetteville home, made famous on the cover of his album, 2014 Forest Hills Drive, would serve as rent-free transitional housing for single mothers in the Cackalack. This could be very beneficial for mothers struggling to provide for their families. Another artist who is similar in his efforts in providing aid to families that are in need is 2 Chainz.

Pretty Girls Like Trap Music

2 Chainz is a Grammy award-winning rapper from College Park, Georgia. I came across this artist over the years with many of his hit singles being blasted on the speakers in my car or in my house, but his fourth album *Pretty Girls Like Trap Music* was the summer trap album of 2017. He has received many BET Awards and BET Hip-Hop Awards and a Grammy. In his philanthropic work, he supports groups like the Hip-Hop Summit Action Network, Voto Latino, and TRU Foundation. Hip-Hop Summit Action Network (HSAN) was co-founded by Russell Simmons and Dr. Benjamin Chavis and is a non-profit, non-partisan national coalition of Hip-Hop artists, entertainment industry leaders, education advocates, civil rights proponents, and youth leaders united in the belief that hip-hop is an enormously influential agent for social change in education, advocacy, and other societal concerns fundamental to the well-being of at-risk youth throughout the United States. Voto Latino is a developing civic media organization that empowers young Latinos to be agents of change through digital campaigns. The TRU Foundation is 2 Chainz's foundation that focuses on promoting balanced, respectful, and enriched relationships, as well as creating life-changing moments to help build positive outcomes for the young generation. He re-

portedly raised $2 million in 2015 through the sales of his Dab-bin' Santa Ugly Christmas Sweaters, where the money went to buying furniture and paying a year's worth of rent for an unemployed single mother and disabled veteran from his hometown of College Park, Georgia. He also bought a minivan for a family who lost their home in a fire and provided a five-bedroom home for a year to a family of 11. Both 2 Chainz and J. Cole provided ways that can bring aid to the work/life, or in the children's case, school/life balance.

Origins of Stress

Origins of stress within the workplace can stem from work relationships, work roles, a design of the work climate, work design, work/life balance and of course, technology, each of which overlaps and can affect an organization on a micro to macro level. Micro-stress is the smaller, sometimes unnoticed stress that occurs over time (in most cases, you don't even take notice that it's stress). Macro-stress is the larger, more noticeable stresses that occur. Both can have negative and positive forms of stress. In understanding how both stresses can affect the overall organization, it will be easier in implementing a stress audit to find out what area of the organization is causing the most stress amongst employees.

Micro-Stresses come in the negative form of small arguments amongst employees or computer meltdowns, to a positive form such as experiencing an intense work day and it finally coming to an end. They are more frequent and is commonly seen to cause the most stress amongst employees on and off the work site. They have little impact on daily lives, but their effects build up over time, leaving a long-lasting effect on an individual.

Macro-Stresses come in a negative form like an employee getting laid off, or a positive form of someone completing a big project and getting a promotion. They have a heavier initial impact on the individual, and do not happen as frequently. However, these stresses can potentially hold the same threat that micro stress can to an individual over time.

Power

50 Cent is a Queens, New York rapper, actor, businessman, and investor. He was prevalent in my life from 2003 with his *Get Rich or Die Tryin'* album. His hardcore thug rap was catchy but not so hot around my household. I remember going on my elementary school senior trip to the Poconos... just like 50 Cent did when he needed to heal from his near-death experience... and the whole class watched his *Get Rich or Die Tryin'* movie in one of the villas. Now this would've been great if my mother, who can't stand too many curse words, was not the chaperone. All hell broke loose. Let's just say that was one of the highlighted moments of the trip. Anyway, back to 50 Cent. Overtime, his music wasn't as heavily listened too. But that didn't stop him from com-

ing out with the Starz cable TV series *Power*. In his philanthropic works, he supports organizations like Shriners Hospitals for Children, New York Restoration Project, and the G-Unity Foundation. Shriners Hospitals for Children provides the highest quality of care to neuromusculoskeletal conditions, burn injuries, and other special healthcare needs to children and their families. New York Restoration Project (NYRP) is a non-profit organization that brings private resources to spaces that lack adequate municipal support, strengthening New York City's aging infrastructure and creating a healthier environment for those who live in the most densely populated and least green neighborhoods. The G-Unity Foundation is a nonprofit foundation that emphasized the importance of supporting academic institutions, supporting other nonprofit organizations that focus on the academic enrichment of a child, and supporting after-schoolactivities. G-Unity Foundation has worked to lift up impoverished Americans, while 50 Cent has also teamed up with Feeding America to deliver food to hungry children. On a global level, 50 Cent has been called a "Humanitarian Genius" in the UN Dispatch after announcing he would donate a billion meals to the UN World Food Program in 2012. At 10 cents a meal, that meant $100 million in sales of his Street King energy drinks that were provided. He even visited Kenya and Somalia to understand the hunger problems facing those countries. Just like the origins of stress that can be both on a micro and macro level, 50 Cent has impacted many people and the environment on both a small and large scale. His philanthropic acts aide in managing both micro and macro stressors that arise every day.

Engagement
The engaged life
we think + feel nothing when fully engaged
'FLOW'

Relationships
authentic, meaningful, life enhancing connections
The related life

Positive emotion
The pleasant life
feeling good   pleasure   comfort   self esteem
happiness   rapture   warmth
satisfaction   optimism
resilience

Well-being theory
Goal. to increase FLOURISHING
Martin Seligman 2011

Vitality   wellness physical health (not part of theory)

The meaningful life

Meaning
purpose   passion
contribution   fulfilment
motivations   belonging

Achievement
inspired action
The accomplished life   success
goals   mastery

© www.tyresandassociates.com.au

Organizational Stress Management and Positive Psychology go hand in hand. Positive psychology concentrates on positive experiences at three-time points: (1) the past, centering on well-being, contentment and satisfaction; (2) the present, which focuses on concepts such as happiness and flow experiences; (3) the future, with concepts including optimism and hope. Martin Seligman, the founder of Positive Psychology, focused on the study of happiness, flourishing, and what makes life worth living. He created the PERMA Theory as the redesigned version of his Orientations to Happiness theory. The Orientations to Happiness theory used three paths to happiness: pleasure, engagement, and meaning. He later added relationships and accomplishment to the list of elements that contribute to well-being (past time point) and created the acronym PERMA. While the Orientations to Happiness theory is about maximizing happiness through the three factors, in PERMA, well-being is a multi-dimensional construct that is defined by its five components (pleasure, engagement, relationships, meaning, and accomplishment). If all of these factors are working together, it can impact organizational stress reduction as individuals will know how to manage their stressors and positively look at situations and outcomes. Each factor affects an individual on three different levels: subjectively, individually, and in a group.

Mihaly Csikszentmihalyi, the co-founder of Positive Psychology, focused on the concept of flow (present time point). Seligman refers to flow in his theories of happiness. Flow is a very positive psychological state that typically occurs when a person perceives a balance between the challenges associated with a situation and their ability to meet the demands of the challenge and achieve it. Csikszentmihalyi's thoughts on flow are the link between flow and happiness depends on whether the flow producing activity is complex, whether it leads to new challenges and hence to personal and cultural growth. He also focuses on the use of creativity (creating new things, making discoveries, etc.) to encourage happiness, and how it can enhance well-being.

Flow can impact organizational stress reduction because once an employee gets into the mind state of flowing with the balance they have come to understand with their challenges and the job demands, they will work to target achieving those goals. The stressor which may have originally been seen as a negative because of an overwhelming workload, may now be viewed as a positive, because an employee's main target in the end is achievement.

Christopher Peterson, former professor of psychology at the University of Michigan and former director of clinical training, contributed to Positive Psychology with the Values in Action (future time point). The Values in Action (VIA) Classification of Strengths identifies 24 commonly valued positive traits that contribute to fulfillment, individual differences like curiosity, kindness, and hope. The VIA survey assesses the degree to which individuals reflect the 24 strengths of character. This theory can impact organizational stress reduction when people recognize their strengths and use them for things they value, and feel a sense of empowerment. When employees are empowered, their productivity in the workplace is higher and stress reduces as they see value in what they are doing, so stressors are viewed positively.

Positive Psychology can be an effective tool for the management of organizational stress and risk assessment, as it provides different outlooks on how an employee views the nature of their work and what brings value, happiness, and growth. According to Kate Heffron and Ilona Boniwell's book *Positive Psychology: Theory, Research, and Applications*, psychologists would argue that positive psychology should improve work satisfaction by helping people to find authentic involvement, experience states of flow and make genuine contributions in their work; that it should improve organizations and societies by discovering conditions that enhance trust, communication, and altruism; and that it should improve the moral character of society by better understanding and promoting the spiritual impulse.

Psychological Well-Being

Psychological well-being is a subjective term, which is used throughout the health industry as a kind of 'catch-all phrase' meaning contentment, satisfaction with all elements of life, self-actualization (a feeling of having achieved something with one's life), peace and happiness. The areas that contribute to psychological well-being are self-acceptance, personal growth, purpose in life, environmental mastery, autonomy, positive relations with others, and spirituality.

3 Peat

Lil Wayne is a Grammy award-winning New Orleans-based rapper, who came into my life when I was only 6-years-old. I remember seeing him on TV with his bandana, baggy jeans, and a wife beater. My brothers listened to him and watched his videos on BET, and although at the time I did not quite understand what he was talking about, he left an impression on me. I didn't grow to love Lil Wayne until *The Carter 3* album dropped while I was in high school. Although he publicly struggled with many mental health and physical issues as a result of his lifestyle, he has still been a great pillar in the hip-hop community which he depicted in his latest album *Carter 5*. He has many accolades under his belt with a total of 64 awards including, one American Music Award, ten BET Awards, five Grammys, and one MOBO Award. He recently was acknowledged for and received the "I Am Hip-

Hop Award" at the 2018 BET Hip-Hop Awards Show. In his philanthropic works, he supports groups like STOKED, The Motivational Edge, and Tha Carter Fund. STOKED is a community that empowers underserved youth through mentorship and action sports culture. The Motivational Edge is a not-for-profit organization that uses culturally relevant arts as a motivational platform to inspire youth towards academic achievement, self-confidence, and building life skills. Tha Carter Fund is an initiative established by Lil Wayne to strengthen charities that set out to improve the quality of life for people in underserved communities. The fund was established to celebrate the thriving spirit of New Orleans communities after Hurricane Katrina. He has aided many people who have been affected by storms in Haiti and his hometown. When Harrell Park fell victim to Hurricane Katrina and became a parking lot for FEMA trailers, Lil Wayne kicked in $200,000 to help rebuild the park. Today, the park shows off basketball courts, lit fields, and an outdoor pool and track.

Emotional Intelligence

With the focus on organizations to keep the wellness and well-being of each employee as the highest priority, understanding social and biological knowledge is key. Wellness is the overall being of the employee both inside and outside of work. The biological knowledge of emotions can help practitioners with the base of how to counter negative behavioral, emotional, or mental states and uphold more positive states of being. If employees struggle with hormonal imbalances or different biological factors that limit them from properly expressing or understanding emotions, it can cause conflicts without knowledge on how to assist each employee based on their needs so they can be an effective member of the team.

On the social end, socio-cognitive processes act on human development, which is defined as a measurement of achievements by humans through the advancement of knowledge, biological changes, habit formation or other criteria that display changes over time. Socio-cognition focuses on how people process, store, and apply information about other people and situations. According to Kimberly Rogers and Liam Kavanaugh's 2010 study, "Bridging Emotion Research: From Biology to Social Structure," they state that, "social and biological processes can be mutually reinforcing, both structures coexist and use each other to develop understanding.

Emotional intelligence is the ability to recognize, control, and express personal emotions as well as being able to recognize and empathize with emotions of someone else. Intelligence is defined as the ability to acquire knowledge and use it. This knowledge can take form in different aspects of life (physical, mental, emotional, spiritual, work/life, etc.). Looking at it from a larger perspective, a person's intelligence is their understanding of their life and the world around them, and involves understanding their emotions.

Emotional intelligence is useful in managing relationships especially during conflict resolution in the workplace. It aids in predicting the quality of social interactions, the amount of received social support, as well as the extent of satisfaction with social support. When employers recognize behavioral shifts in their employees, they will be able to resolve conflicts without the possibility of the situation escalating. Understanding emotional intelligence can also benefit the psychological, physical, and social state of an individual.

Interpersonal and Intrapersonal Functioning in the Workplace

Interpersonal and intrapersonal functioning in the workplace can take forms in both negative and positive ways. Intrapersonal functioning in the workplace can be seen through emotional intelligence/competence and emotional regulation. Emotional regulation refers to the process in which individuals choose which emotions they express, relative to those they experience, in either a controlled or an automatic response. People normally regulate their emotions and emotional displays to conform to norms and expectations of the workplace, as well as with job role demands. Emotional regulation in the workplace can be a negative practice. It is linked with an increase in stress levels and a decrease in job satisfaction. It is also commonly seen that emotional regulation usually results in both faking positive and hiding negative emotions, which can cause an imbalance in the well-being of an employee. However, handling emotions in the workplace to fit the professional demeanor of an organization is necessary.

Interpersonal functioning in the workplace can be noted with the Resilience Theory, Appraisal Theories, organizational citizenship, emotional intelligence/emotional competence, and conflict resolution.

Resilience Theory: This theory is commonly seen amongst families and understanding adolescents, however it has been very useful in the workplace. It guides data analytic strategies and can inform the design of intervention by defining strategies to enhance promotive factors. With the focus of employee wellness and well-being in organizations, and the crossover with positive psychology, the resilience theory in the workplace is a new phenomenon as it focuses on the positive aspects of supporting resilience and how to achieve it. According to the American Heart Association, "the existing resilience literature suggests that resilience training programs in the workplace have low to moderate, but statistically significant effects on a broad range of physical, mental health, well-being, psychosocial and work performance outcomes." Resilience training is also a new tool that organizations use to promote employee health. Resilience training programs may be a primary prevention tactic for employees to reduce stress and depression in the workplace. However, in order to really understand and define the resilience theory in the workplace, more research needs to be conducted. The theory falls short because it doesn't consider how long it takes for employees to revert to the mental processes and behaviors before the issue or crisis took place.

Appraisal Theories: Appraisal theorists believe that thought and emotion are largely inseparable, that emotions arise from the individual's perceptions—its appraisals—of environmental changes that are relevant to its well-being. In the workplace, many factors take place when it comes down to dealing with conflicts. It is often seen that in the workplace, many people use emotional regulation or a carefully thought out process to best deal with an issue that arises with much respect of their surroundings and keeping their job. Language, culture, maturation, and life experiences are forces that make emotions and their associated appraisals accessible and automatic. In terms of hip-hop, when emotions arise, artists take to their craft of expressing themselves. Sometimes this can be taken negatively or positively depending on how they present their emotions and depending on the perspectives of those observing their work.

Organizational Citizenship: Organizational Citizenship Behaviors (OCB) are those which are voluntary and above the normal day-to-day behaviors that not only contribute, but are necessary for organizational success. It is based around how each employee views their organization and their involvement in it. There are five categories that constitute to organizational citizenship behavior: altruism, helping of an individual coworker on a task without expecting anything in return; courtesy, alerting others in the organization about changes that may affect their work, being considerate or polite; conscientious, carrying out one's duties beyond the minimum requirements, going above and beyond normal expectations; sportsmanship, refraining from complaining about trivial matters, staying in good spirits even when something creates a considerable amount of frustration; and civic virtue, participating in the governance of the organization, representing the organization in a positive way. Leaders should always look for employees who exhibit these behaviors, as well as demonstrate these behaviors in their own practices.

Conflict Resolution: Conflict resolution can prevent future issues from arising or further damage from occurring. How you resolve the conflict and the way you do so, by staying professional and efficient at all times. Conflict resolution is seen to take form in five different strategies:

Forcing: the system when one party forces another to accept a particular position, very high assertive behavior and low cooperativeness, so a win-lose orientation is adopted which may result in negative work behavior.

Smoothing: the system of avoiding conflict, low assertive behavior and high cooperativeness. Differences are not emphasized amongst either party, and points common to both parties are highlighted.

Compromising: the system with a give-and-take method of resolving a conflict. Each party gives up something that the other party wants. This style may result in positive work behavior and attitudes.

Confronting/Collaborating: the system which engages a lot of interaction, high on both assertive and cooperative behaviors. Involves information sharing, openness, and clarification of issues on the point of conflict to reach an acceptable solution.

Withdrawing: the system to refrain from or completely ignore conflict, low on both assertive and cooperative behaviors. The style has the tendency to cause counterproductive work behaviors.

Uncle Snoop

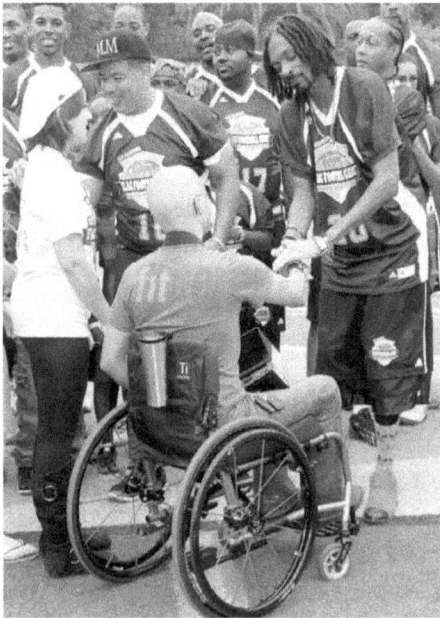

Snoop Dogg is a rapper, songwriter, singer, record producer, television personality, and actor from Long Beach, California. This hip-hop icon has won over 27 awards including one American Music Award and one BET Award. Snoop Dogg was not always known as Uncle Snoop to the rising generation. I first encountered Snoop Dogg with his song, "Gin & Juice" being played over the loud speaker at one of my family's barbecues. The smooth hip-hop melody and Snoop Dogg's flow was perfect for the summer night vibe. His role as Rodney from the *Baby Boy* film featuring actors Tyrese Gibson and Taraji P. Henson, was one of my favorites. He turned his bad boy image around in so many ways that he is truly a wise

OG of hip-hop culture. In his philanthropic work, he supports groups like Habitat for Humanity, Save a Life Foundation, and Snoop Youth Football League. Habitat for Humanity brings people together to build, homes, communities, and hope around the world. Snoop Dogg auctioned off 'An Hour with Snoop' which allowed someone to hang with him in the studio as funds were raised for Habitat For Humanity's Operation Home Delivery Fund. The Save a Life Foundation is a foundation focused on bringing awareness about cardiac health and health screenings to youth. Snoop Dogg held a charity basketball game at his former school which helped benefit the school and his Save a Life-Foundation. He also coaches at his Snoop Youth Football League (SYFL), which was established in 2005 from gaining inspiration from his sons who loved the game. He created the league to help children avoid the gang lifestyle that almost took over his life and his music career. Snoop also devoted his time to help deliver 1,500 turkeys in Inglewood with the Mayor. In terms of business, Snoop Dogg is a true icon in his transition over many entertainment platforms. In the focus of conflict resolution, he has turned his bad boy persona around and taken on the role of Uncle Snoop to help mentor and nurture many artists that have come after him or looked up to him. He emphasizes the need to end violence and hate amongst artistry in hip-hop because the goal is to strive for a more positive future.

Organizational Stress Management Treatment Plans/ Strategies

Organizational stress management adds value to an overall organization by showing employees that their well-being is important and that they are valued by their organization. Observation of stress in leadership and employees, as well as involvement in solving it are essential in combating occupational stress.

Organizational stress management can take forms in many ways. Many strategies of stress reduction of an individual nature are: psycho-pharmacological interventions (the prescription of medicines), psychotherapy, and various relaxation techniques (i.e., transcendental meditation, Zen meditation, autogenic training, and biofeedback). The effects of these stress reductive strategies happen sooner rather than later, since they are directing the body's chemistry. However, these fast results may not be long-lasting. In any form, taking medication may affect different parts or organs of the body in excess. Aside from body changes, it can also influence personality and mental stability. In a more drastic turn, medication can cause addictive habits and even death if the medication is not properly calibrated for that person.

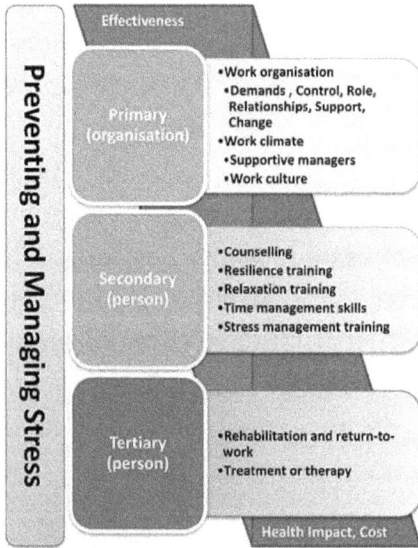

Occupational Stress Management can occur on the organizational and individual level, and by finding balance in self and by providing ways to prevent or minimize stress through their hiring process or job demands. General occupational stress reduction measures refer to activities such as: reducing work of individuals or even implementing an intervention, simplifying procedures and tasks of different activities, enabling the individual to express unpleasant feelings about their condition. The strengths of these strategies have longer lasting effects at building up the employee's confidence in helping them find balance within their career and personal life. Another strength is that the organization may start these strategies from the very beginning, so stress levels are high as an organization who did not implement stress reducers in their hiring process. This strategy, however, is time-consuming and may take longer for effects to show.

In conclusion, to develop an approach for stress management, one must know the levels of stress. In understanding the different levels of stress, you can categorize different workplace stressors, and measure their intensity and frequency in a stress audit. A stress audit is a tool that can be used to identify stress in different areas of business. This is where Positive Psychology can be heavily present in the approach to organizational stress management. In "Positive Psychology: Theory, Research, and Applications," Jane Henry proposed practices for a positive organization that include: job variety, intrinsic motivation, confidence, creativity, strengths work, meta perspective, flow, participatory working practices, an open climate, empowerment and self-organization. With these subgroups, it would be easy for you to assess these areas in an organization to see how often these stressors are evident in the workplace, if they are seen as negative or positive stressors, and how these areas can improve. Positive organizing is the term used to describe the links between positive psychology and organizational theory. In general terms, it refers to the generative dynamics in and of the organizations that enable individuals, groups and organizations to prosper. This information can guide the model for stress management in targeting areas that are lacking or seen to have prominently negative stressors.

"I Used to Love H.E.R."

Common is a Grammy award-winning recording artist, actor, poet, and film producer from Chicago, Illinois. I previously spoke about Common's song "I Used to Love H.E.R." as the song that best described my love for hip-hop. But what I did not get into was how this artist influenced me. I grew up on a lot of Common's music and never realized how long he has been in the hip-hop game (1987 to present...wayyyyyyyyyy before I was even thought of). One of the most powerful songs he released that really touched me was "Glory" featuring John Legend, the main song for the film *Selma*. He also starred in the film, as well as other major films with co-stars like Queen Latifah (*Just Wright*), Keanu Reeves (*John Wick: Chapter 2*), Denzel Washington (*American Gangster*), and with Alicia Keys and Taraji P. Henson (*Smokin' Aces*). Common's philanthropic efforts fall nothing short of his career. He supports groups like PETA, Get Schooled Foundation, and the Common Ground Foundation. PETA is an animal rights organization throughout the world with over 6.5 million followers, in which Common has appeared in many of their ads. The Get Schooled Foundation is a foundation that empowers and engages young people providing them with tools and inspiration they need to get an education. The Common Ground Foundation was created by Common to serve as an inspiration for equality, opportunity, and hope amongst underprivileged youth. He has also raised money for HIV/AIDS research.

Expectations for a Health Psychology Consultant

The expectations for a health psychology consultant working with an organization in need of assistance, is to provide the organization with the necessary information and resources needed to ensure a healthy and safe environment, and healthy employees. Health psychology consultants can work with management and leaders to impact unhealthy work environments in the organization to understand exactly where the main issues are housed. An unhealthy work environment has poor communication, uncivil behavior, disrespect, resistance to change, lack of vision/leadership, lack of trust, lack of professional growth, and conflict with values. Health psychology consultants can implement or suggest changes that need to be made in the organization to ensure employee satisfaction and minimize employee stress. They are to provide organizations with a balance of positive psychology practices and public health awareness.

Greater cooperation between positive psychology and public health might help promote positive mental health in new ways that can improve overall health. Positive psychology shares similar focuses as other disciplines of psychology like positive emotions, positive individual traits, positive relationships, and enabling institutions. In all these areas, public health is very prevalent in that research is being conducted or educational systems are being implemented to raise awareness on positive mental health and overall well-being.

T.I. is a great example of our millennial hip-hop consultant. As a teen growing up, T.I. was my celebrity crush, a permanent screensaver on my cell phone in high school. T.I or Tip Harris, is a rapper, actor, entrepreneur, author, record producer, record executive, and song-writer from Atlanta, Georgia. Aside from listening to the music artists my older brothers played, he was primarily how I got hooked onto listening to trap music with his "Rubber Band Man" from his 2003 *Trap Muzik* album. His southern twang and bad boy demeanor (especially in his role in *ATL* co-starring Lauren London) melted my young school girl heart. However, I didn't realize how exactly I would grow to respect him on a business level. Over the years, T.I. has evolved from being known as the "Rubber Band Man" into an elite businessman through which anyone can recall was his greatest Grand Hustle. He is particularly known for his exquisite vocabulary and his constant words of wisdom, which he so graciously presents us with on his television shows like *T.I & Tiny: Family Hustle* and *The Grand Hustle*, and television features like *Hip Hop Squares*. He has excelled in both the music and film industry with his collaborations on camera and/or behind the scenes, such as with films *American Gangster* and *Hustle & Flow*. With his experiences in the industry and in the streets, T.I. continuously thrives on teaching those around him the true meaning of hard work in being an entrepreneur. Pharrell recognizes him as the "Jay-Z of the South." In 2010, he was named the Global Creative Consultant of Remy Martin Cognac, in which the partnership would include collaborative projects and focus on continuing the work of his philanthropic efforts in his K.I.N.G. Foundation. He also is another artist-owner of TIDAL. T.I. built his business empire from the ground up, and like most entrepreneurs who want to continue to expand their empire, he searched for skilled individuals to join his team. During 2018, he offered the opportunity for millennials like myself to compete in what he called "The Grand Hustle" to claim a spot within his multi-million-dollar company, as well as secure a six-figure salary. Now, who can really deny that experience? He pushed each candidate through challenges and offered mentorship to prepare them for the career they desired. Each week a candidate was eliminated, and in the end a New York native and member of the Alpha Kappa Alpha Sorority, Krystal Garner, secured her crown as the Queen of Grand Hustle. T.I is a true hip-hop entrepreneurial consultant.

So, let's take a long ride and unwind…

The sun is setting, as it touches the road going down I-97 on this summer evening… the car in cruise control moving at 60 mph… my mind is clear and my heart listens as Lauryn Hill speaks in the background

"Sometimes it seems
We'll touch that dream
But things come slow or not at all
And the ones on top, won't make it stop
So convinced that they might fall
Let's love ourselves and we can't fail
To make a better situation
Tomorrow, our seeds will grow
All we need is dedication
Let me tell ya that

Everything is everything
What is meant to be, will be
After winter, must come spring
Change, it comes eventually"

-"Everything is Everything" by Lauryn Hill

The Hip-Hop Workplace

In today's society, we constantly see changes in the nature of work. The workplace is transitioning into a workforce that is more urbanized and advanced. Thanks to technology and the changes in society, the changes in the workforce is happening swifter than ever with more millennials being hired and mixed amongst Generation X and Baby Boomers. *Military.com* based an article on the influences of hip-hop in the workplace, especially amongst African Americans.

Ben Sherold, president and CEO of Diversity Search Group speaks his thoughts on millennials and the hip-hop workplace. "African Americans of my generation – 45, 50, 55 years old – are probably more conservative than the mainstream media gives us credit for. We think things should be 'professional.' Young people's definition of 'professional' is different." The article discusses topics in which hip-hop can influence the workplace: a person's style, mental state, and attitude.

A person's style consists of their personal choices with the clothes they wear, the hairstyle they choose to wear, and the language or slang they speak. In society today, you can see millennials going to job interviews not dressed in the traditional suit and tie, or garments suitable for women to wear in the workplace. In the *Military.com* article, Sherold stated, "When I interview young people now, I have to remind them how to dress... They don't seem to think their appearance has any impact on an interviewer. They talk in rap slang... it takes a while, but eventually they realize you can't really communicate that way." The hairstyles recently have taken a turn for very expressive and modern. This could mean different colors, different cuts, and designs.

A person's mental state is also influenced by hip-hop. With millennials being more expressive and truer to themselves, their mindset is focused on finding a balance between their hip-hop culture and corporate culture. Sometimes it is seen that hip-hop is not fully appropriate for the corporate world. However, there are many multi-billion-dollar companies that openly and successfully accept hip-hop into their organizational culture. An example that was given in the *Military.com* article was with Coca-Cola USA, Sprite soft drinks. Sprite became the fastest-growing soft drink brand in the country because they created authentic ads that related to the hip-hop community. Sprite featured artists in their commercials like Method Man and Q-Tip, and their most notable slogan "Obey your thirst" was coined by rapper Grand Puba, a member of the group Brand Nubian in a freestyle rap.

Finally, a person's attitude can reflect hip-hop. Many iconic members of the hip-hop community have used hip-hop to fuel the dreams and goals. Carol Lewis, president and CEO of CSL Image Consulting, gave her view on hip-hop culture and the attitude in the *Military.com* article. She stated, "Plenty of talented, creative individuals come from that culture... They're fearless, zealous and they want something better for their lives. They use their street skills in the workplace. They're willing to make a deal at all costs or relocate anywhere if it means getting on the fast track. They're natural salespeople. They look at all different angles of a situation, and they take great risks. It's a bold attitude."

Jay-Z and P. Diddy are two of the most popular icons in the hip-hop community that have used the rugged, grind nature of hip-hop to transform their careers.

The hip-hop workplace can have many benefits as well as many drawbacks. However, like with all things, there needs to be a balance. A good example of balance can be the National Basketball Association. Over the years, there was controversy on the appearance of players influenced by hip-hop. However, they have now been able to find the kind of balance to include hip-hop within reasonable matters. According to the *Military.com* article, "Many athletes and white-collar workers reclaim their hip-hop sensibility off the court and outside the office."

Being that the workplace is very prominent in remote areas, this is the greatest time to talk about how the hip-hop workplace can be seen from behind the computer screens. Being an entrepreneur can mean getting into any form of business even if it means getting into the digital world.

Nipsey Hussle is a rapper from Los Angeles, California who built his brand from the ground up. My first interaction with Nipsey Hussle was during the release of his major-label debut *Victory Lap*. After listening to his long-awaited album (a decade to be exact) and attending his concert at Irvington Plaza in New York, June of 2018, I became a bigger fan of Nipsey. What intrigues me most about this icon is his drive and hunger through his music and the outside world. He made a name for himself in the digital world through cryptocurrencies. He initially invested in Bitcoin back in 2013, and now he is an ambassador and beneficiary of the industry, owning a stake in an Amsterdam crypto company called Follow Coin. Bitcoin spiked recently by hitting an all-time high of $10,000 per coin in the beginning months of 2018. His hustle was seen far and wide by artists like Jay-Z back in 2013 for his *Crenshaw* project, when he sold his mixtape for $100 per copy and Jay-Z brought 100 copies, to even those who work for him at a strip mall in California that holds his clothing line The Marathon Clothing. Nipsey Hussle is the epitome of a millennial hip-hop entrepreneur.Hip-Hop is everywhere... Don't you see it?

Finale

As we come to a close, all I can think about are these lyrics....

"Ready or not, here I come, you can't hide
Gonna find you and take it slowly
Ready or not, here I come, you can't hide
Gonna find you and make you want me"

"Ready or Not" by Fugees

Ready or Not, the time for you to impact your next organization or boss is NOW.

As you see, Industrial Organizational Psychology is complex but many of the concepts can overlap in your personal life. If it's not hip-hop..., that's cool... (Allllllllthoughhhhhh, you are missing out on some historical moments with hip-hop). Just stay true to self and always open your mind to acquiring knowledge. Who says you can't teach an old dog new tricks?! (*sighs, rolls eyes*)

Change is dependent on you, and in order to do so in an effective and successful way, you must have the knowledge and proper tools. As an IOP advisor, you're damn near the right hand to the organization. So, ACT LIKE IT!!

Who knows... Maybe you will be your own boss one day
wink wink

BOSS UP, YA HEARD!

Now let that Hov play out...

Beat drops

Hova Song (Outro) by Jay-Z starts to play in the background

Jay speaks

"Who ever thought young Shawn Carter would change the game?

Used to rap to the raindrops off my window pane

Duckin' the plain cops, pushin' endo and 'caine

At the kitchen table late night, no pen, just my brain

First album niggas love me cause they thought I was poor

Guess I'm successful; industry don't love me no more

Well I'm the same nigga from your corner, bubblin' raw

Skully tilted, pants saggin', damn near touchin' the floor

And I come with doo-rags to your so-called awards

T-shirt with my chain out like fuck y'all

Retrospect ain't been the same since I lost my dad

He's still alive, but still fuck you, don't cross my path

A&R's had me feelin' like Moss in the draft

So I turned the league out with "Reasonable Doubt"

Get your CDs out, let's go, song for song

I'm the illest nigga doin' it 'til y'all prove me wrong

Do you believe?

It's Hova the God, uhh, uhh, uhh..."

References

American Heart Association. (n.d.) Resilience in the Workplace. Retrieved February 18, 2018, from http://www.heart.org/idc/groups/heart-public/@wcm/@cep/documents/downloadable/ ucm_496855.pdf

Bauer, T. & Erdogan, B. (2012). An Introduction to Organizational Behavior. Retrieved from http://2012books.lardbucket.org/pdfs/an-introduction-to-organizational-behavior-v1.1.pdf

Bennis, Warren (2007). The Challenges of Leadership in the Modern World, American Psychologist, Vol. 62, No. 1, pp. 2-5. Retrieved from EbscoHost Academic Search Complete.

Buckingham, M. & Goodall, A. (2015). Reinventing Performance Management, Harvard Business Review. Retrieved from https://hbr.org/2015/04/reinventing-performance-management

Cherry, Kendra (2016). The Asch Conformity Experiments. Retrieved from: https:// www.verywell.com/the-asch-conformity-experiments-2794996

Ciotti, Gregory (2016). 15 Customer Service Skills that Every Employee Needs. Retrieved from: https://www.helpscout.net/blog/customer-service-skills/

Creekmore, B. (2015, August 13). Can hip-hop help people cope with mental illness? Retrieved February 12, 2018, from https://www.sovhealth.com/mental-health/hip-hop-help-people-cope- mental-illness/

Creswell, J. W. (2014). Research Design: Qualitative, Quantitative, and Mixed Method Approaches. Sage Publications

'Drop the Mic'. Retrieved January 30, 2018, from http://www.latimes.com/entertainment/music/ la-et-st-method-man-on-tv-20171006-story.html

Fox, A. (2016, October 14). Hip-Hop Artists Have Been Writing About Mental Health For Decades. Retrieved February 12, 2018, from https://www.huffingtonpost.com/entry/mental-health-hip-hop_us_57fbca3ae4b068ecb5e087a1

Gardiner, John Jacob (2006). Transactional, Transformational, And Transcendent Leadership - Metaphors Mapping The Evolution Of The Theory And Practice Of Governance. Leadership Review, Vol.6. Retrieved from http://www.leadershipreview.org/2006spring/Article3.pdf

Greenburg, Z. O. (2017, September 27). Diddy And Russell Simmons: Wisdom From Hip-Hop's Top Business Minds. Retrieved February 01, 2018, from https://www.forbes.com/sites/zackomalleygreenburg/2017/09/27/diddy-and-russell-simmons-wisdom-from-hip-hops-top- business-minds/#7613e2872890

Heffron, K. & Boniwell, I. Positive Psychology: Theory, Research and Application, Open Book University Press, 2011 (Please Read Chapter 1-2, 11). Retrieved from Touro Library eBooks.

Karlgaard, Rich (2004). Peter Drucker On Leadership. Retrieved from: http://www.forbes.com/ 2004/11/19/cz_rk_1119drucker.html

Kennedy, G. D. (2015, November 05). Bad Boy For Life: A look back at the rap empire Sean Puff Daddy Combs built. Retrieved February 04, 2018, from http://www.latimes.com/ entertain-

ment/music/posts/la-et-ms-sean-p-diddy-combs-bad-boy-enter-
tainment- retrospective-20151005-story.html

Lerman, R. I., & Schmidt, S. R. (n.d.). An overview of economic, social, and demographic trends affecting the US labor market.
U.S. Department of Labor. Retrieved from http://www.dol.gov/
oasam/programs/history/herman/reports/futurework/confer-
ence/trends/trendsI.html

Linley, Alex P., Woolston, Linda, & Biswas-Diener, Robert
(2009). Strengths Coaching With Leaders, International Coaching Psychology Review, Vol. 4, No. 1, March 2009.

McInerney, Sarah (2011). Steve Jobs: an unconventional leader. Retrieved from http:// www.executivestyle.com.au/
steve-jobs-an-unconventional-leader-1lcmo

Meanthat (2013). What Is Organizational Theory | Introduc-
tion To Organisations | MeanThat [Video file]. Retrieved from
https://www.youtube.com/watch?v=4AM10-uNabA

Military.com. (n.d.). The Hip-Hop Workplace. Retrieved February 25, 2018, from https:// www.military.com/veteran-jobs/ca-
reer-advice/on-the-job/hip-hop-workplace.html

Mullins, L. J., & Christy, G. (2016). *Management &organisatio-
nalbehaviour*. Harlow: Pearson.

National Research Council. 1999. The Changing Nature of
Work: Implications for Occupational Analysis. Washington, DC:
The National Academies Press. doi: 10.17226/9600.

Nigel Marsh: How to Make Work-Life Balance Work, TED Talk.
[Video file]. Retrieved from http://www.ted.com/talks/nigel_
marsh_how_to_make_work_life_balance_work?language=en
(10:01)

O'Meara, B., & Petzall, S. B. (2013). Handbook of Strategic Recruitment and Selection: A Systems Approach. United Kingdom: Emerald Group Publishing Limited. Retrieved from eBook Collection (EBSCOhost) database in the Touro library

Patterson, V. L. (n.d.). Engaging Hip-Hop Leadership: Diversity, Counter-Hegemony and Glorified

Perez, T. E. (2015, July). Rising to the challenge of a 21st-century workforce. Monthly Labor Review. 1-4. Retrieved from EBSCO multi-search database in the TUW Library.

Rogers, K. & Kavanagh, L. (2010).Bridging emotion research: From biology to social structure. Social Psychology Quarterly, 73(4), 333-334. Retrieved from EBSCO Multi-search database in the Touro library.

Solomon, Micah (2013). Building Customer Loyalty the Hard (And Only) Way. Retrieved from: http://www.forbes.com/sites/groupthink/2013/07/22/building-customer-loyalty-the-hard-and-only-way/

Srivastava, K. (2009). Urbanization and mental health. Retrieved February 12, 2018, from https://www.ncbi.nlm.nih.gov/pmc/articles/PMC2996208/

www.ingramcontent.com/pod-product-compliance
Lightning Source LLC
Chambersburg PA
CBHW070923030426
42336CB00014BA/2519